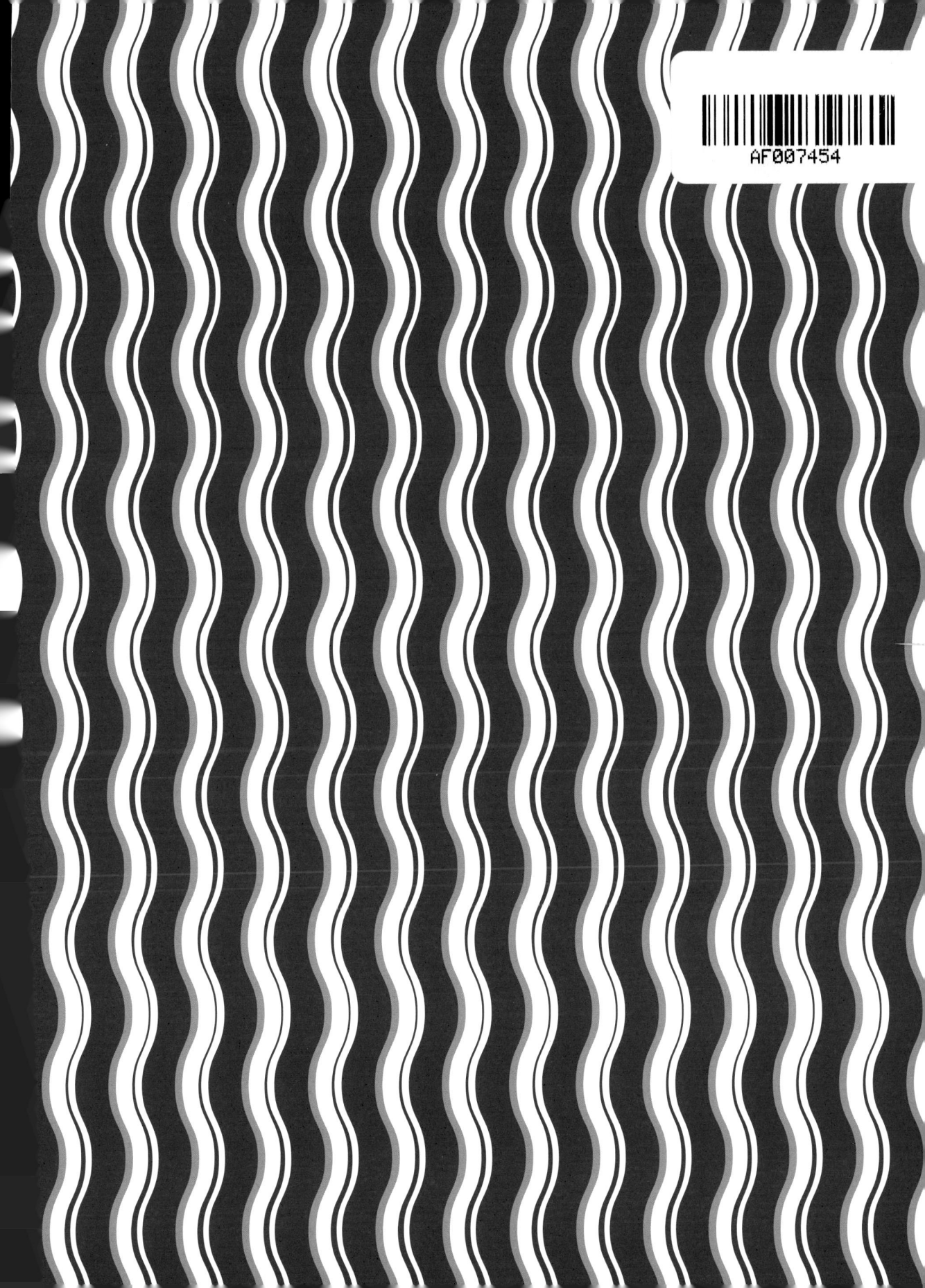

LONG DAY? COOK THIS.

LONG DAY? COOK THIS.
EASY EAST ASIAN RECIPES WITH A TWIST

JUSTIN TSANG

EBURY PRESS

Dedicated to my beautiful wife,
Mimi Paul.
Here's to spending the rest of
our lives together.

And to my best friend,
Harry Hood.
We started this food journey together –
I'll try my best to finish it.
May you rest in peace (1994–2018).

INTRODUCTION 08
MY STORE CUPBOARD 15
RICE (AND HOW TO COOK IT) 20

JUST WOKEN UP?
BREAKFAST & BRUNCH 24

NEED TO EAT NOW?
QUICK & EASY 54

FORGOT TO DO A SHOP?
STORE CUPBOARD STAPLES 86

KEEPING IT LIGHT?
FRESH & HEALTHY(ISH) 110

FEEDING A CROWD?
DISHES TO SHARE 142

FEELING HUNGOVER?
SIMPLE & COMFORTING 170

WANT TO TREAT YO' SELF?
SOMETHING SPECIAL 202

COOK'S NOTES 230
INDEX 232
ABOUT THE AUTHOR 237
ACKNOWLEDGEMENTS 238

HEY THERE!

Long days are a daily occurrence for many of us – whether it's because of work, family, personal responsibilities or other unexpected complications . . . the list goes on! But, for me, the best cure for an especially long day (whatever the cause) is always a properly delicious home-cooked meal.

When we're feeling run down or tired, we can often stray into the ease and convenience of ordering our favourite takeaway, eating ready meals or just repeating the same old unimaginative recipes. My hope is that with this book, you'll discover a way to cook banging meals that will never be a chore – even at the end of a long day.

Born and raised in North London to Hong Kong immigrant parents, food was my family's way of preserving our heritage and culture in a foreign land that hadn't yet strayed beyond takeaway-style food. After moving to the UK, my parents opened a Chinese buffet in 1993 and it soon became our second home. I spent many afternoons and evenings there after long days at school, doing homework and, of course, eating! This was the start of my obsession with the only world my family felt comfortable in: food. Those long, arduous hours waiting for my parents as an already impatient and hyperactive kid meant I would roam the kitchen, annoying as many people I could, particularly the chefs. I was fascinated by the roaring fires used to heat the woks and the noise of the fans that resembled a jet engine. Before I knew it, I wanted to cook, eat and learn.

While I was growing up, though, I got caught between two worlds: my family in Hong Kong saw me as English, while my friends in England saw me as Chinese. In school, I would be teased for my home-cooked Chinese packed lunches – consisting of soup, rice and dishes none of my classmates had ever seen before. Feeling like the odd one out only made me want to eat pasta, pizza and chicken nuggets! But as I got older, I slowly grew to understand my true identity: I'm neither English nor Chinese, I'm somewhere in between. I learnt to embrace my heritage and the variety of food that comes with it, as well as learning about food from other corners of the world because, to me, that tells us more about different cultures than anything else.

In many ways, food was my escape from any tough times I was going through; it had the ability to change my mood. Food was always there. I could almost call it an obsession. I spent countless hours as an 18-year-old watching Food Network rather than the latest drop of *Skins*, *Big Brother* or *Love Island*, and today I watch endless YouTube travel and food culture vlogs . . . I even watch food videos while I eat (is that strange?).

Having spent many years as a kid in the restaurant, of course the natural direction to take in life was to get in there and make it my profession. Soon after university, I moved into the kitchen where my love of food began: my parents' restaurant. While working and training there, I realised that many of the older generation were stubborn in their traditions. I'd experiment with traditional recipes and add a little modern flair, but had nowhere to share my creations – that's why I decided to share my passion online. All too often I had heard from friends how a long day of work resulted in an evening meal that had to prioritise time while sacrificing flavour and enjoyment. Why should that be the case? Food is not a chore and never should be, so I chose to focus on creating easy, quick and delicious recipes that could be put together after a hard day with no stress. Each of my videos starts with me coming through the door and ends with me eating (usually on the sofa), as an honest representation of most people's evening routine. I love that through my social channels I can share the recipes I create and enjoy eating myself (as well as my addiction to the mini basketball set-up in my kitchen . . . though I still rarely get it in).

A few decades ago, the majority of the East Asian cuisine available in the UK was Cantonese. There was a lack of exposure to other regions and countries that share the same ingredients but rely on different traditions and use alternative techniques. Vietnamese food, for instance, is heavy on rice and noodles like Chinese food, but incorporates lots of fresh herbs and veg, fish sauce and citrus. On the other side of the spectrum, Korean cuisine features a huge array of fermented foods like kimchi and gochujang, plus they have an obsession with spice and, perhaps surprisingly, cheese! Japanese food instead values simplicity, bringing the main ingredients to the forefront and making those shine. I made it my mission to learn about everything I could, and to celebrate both parts of my identity.

Over the years, I've gradually honed both my Eastern and Western influences and created my own cooking style, which is what you'll find in this book – traditional cooking techniques made easy, with lots of East and Southeast Asian foundations and flavours paired with Western ingredients. Check out my **Spicy Chicken Escalope Sando** on page 70 or **Carbonara Instant Noodles** on page 93, which twists a traditional carbonara with ramen noodles and nori seaweed. Spotting similarities between different cuisines and swapping them around is something I absolutely love to do (sorry, Italians).

I think East Asian food can get a bad rap for being complicated, but I focus on making my recipes super accessible. I'm a laid-back cook, so you'll find quick and simple meals in this book that will make sure cooking for yourself or others after a long day is self-care, not a chore. Through these recipes, I hope you'll come to see how easy it is to pull together a meal with ingredients found at your local supermarket, with perhaps one or two East Asian ingredients you can have on hand in your store cupboard or freezer (see overleaf) tying everything together, to create a dish you'll cook again and again. My cooking is all about big flavours, with no stress.

I hope that with these recipes, you find loads of new weekly staples that will not only elevate your repertoire but also open your imagination to a world of new and accessible recipes – all with a twist! There's something here for everybody, so whatever floats your boat and whatever situation you're in, give it a try and, most of all, don't stress. Get the tunes on and enjoy it!

Justin xx

MY STORE CUPBOARD

Many store cupboard staples form the base flavours of my cooking and show who I am in the kitchen – think of it like a wardrobe: you can tell a lot by the clothing you wear. Mine features many sauces and condiments and, most importantly, a never-ending drawer of noodles! Below I've explained a bit about some of the key ingredients I use. The more specialist items can be found in supermarkets or East Asian shops. I encourage you to try to find them, as they will take your cooking to the next level.

CORNFLOUR

Cornflour is a great gluten-free alternative to flour and is the most common ingredient used for thickening East Asian sauces. Similarly to flour, it needs liquid to activate it. Mixing together equal parts cornflour and water creates a slurry, which can be stirred into your sauce towards the end of cooking. It does have a tendency to form lumps, so pour it in slowly while gently stirring. It also reacts to heat, so reduce the heat to low or off when pouring, then slowly heat until you reach your desired consistency.

Cornflour is not only used for thickening, though. The traditional Chinese technique called 'velveting' uses cornflour to marinate meats or fish (and even tofu) to create a seal, locking in the juices and tenderising the meat. Cornflour can also be used in batters for deep-frying, for example when making salt and pepper squid (see page 207). It's lighter, crispier and quicker to cook than a regular flour batter.

DASHI POWDER

An integral ingredient that forms the base of many Japanese recipes, dashi powder is made from dried and shaved bonito (a fish similar to tuna) and kombu seaweed. It adds a wonderful umami, slightly salty and smoky note to dishes. Think of it as the Japanese chicken stock cube. If you have it, use it.

DOUBANJIANG

This useful Chinese paste is made from fermented broad beans and chillies and has deep nutty notes, spiciness, saltiness and umami.

FRIED SHALLOTS

Shop-bought fried shallots are a life-saver – they stay super crispy in the cupboard for months and save you hours of prep time. Most of the time, there's no reason to make your own. You can find them in a lot of high-street supermarkets, but fried onions are interchangeable and also widely available.

GOCHUGARU

These Korean red pepper (i.e. chilli) flakes are a dark, bold red; they are coarser than chilli powder and much finer than Western chilli flakes. The seeds are removed, which means they have a medium spice kick and bring a great deep red colour to dishes. Use as a condiment or ingredient in recipes – they're super versatile and can be used just like regular chilli flakes. Try sprinkling them over pizza or pasta.

GOCHUJANG

The Korean cousin of doubanjiang, it's thicker, darker, sweeter and less salty.

JAPANESE MAYONNAISE

Made with egg yolks only, richer, more acidic, creamier and less gloopy than regular Western mayo. It also tends to be seasoned with sweeter vinegars and MSG, unlike regular mayo, which is usually unseasoned. Kewpie is a widely available brand and my go-to.

INSTANT NOODLES

There are so many variations of instant noodles that, believe it or not, really differ from country to country. Different portion sizes, different ingredients and, most importantly, different widths of noodle (thinner or thicker) and texture. These will change the outcome of recipes – not by much, but they are noticeable! Which one you use is up to you, so choose whatever you like, try them out and find your favourite!

CHINESE AND JAPANESE: These are the most common and widely available type of instant noodles. They cook in 2–3 minutes, are pale yellow in colour and medium thick. The texture is soft, but still has a bite. Brands like Nissin are my go-to here, which can be found in most supermarkets.

KOREAN: My favourite and recommended type of noodle. Korean instant noodles are usually larger portion sizes, have a brighter yellow colour and are the thickest noodle on the market. They stay al dente for longer and have a much better chew, in my opinion. Brands like Shin Ramyun, Samyang and Jin are perfect.

THAI: The smallest of the noodles, with a yellow-brown colour and soft texture. They cook in seconds and are perfect for noodle salads. Brands like Mama are my choice.

Like pasta, cooking instant noodles for the right amount of time will make a huge difference to your eating experience. To preserve the chewiness and texture of the noodles, cooking them al dente is important. With all noodles, I recommend cooking them for 1 minute less than the time stated on the packet instructions, especially if you're making noodle soup, as the noodles will keep cooking while you eat due to the residual heat. Nobody likes a soggy noodle.

MSG

Monosodium glutamate is a seasoning that adds umami savouriness to any dish and is commonly used in East and Southeast Asian cooking, as part of a holy trinity along with sugar and salt. It's usually the final seasoning, used to bring out the flavours of the ingredients. While it is a naturally occurring substance found in foods such as mushrooms, seaweed, cheese and fermented hot sauces, it has a bad rap in the West. Though there is no evidence it is addictive or damaging, just like salt or sugar, moderation is key. It's not a cheat code, it's a necessity.

NORI

These dried and roasted sheets of seaweed are most commonly used to make sushi rolls. Usually sold in large squares, they can be cut down or sliced depending on what the recipe calls for. You can also buy them salted and flavoured, in smaller sizes. I often use them in thin strips to garnish dishes. To make these, use a pair of scissors to cut the nori lengthways into quarters. Stack the sheets, then cut them into very thin strips.

OYSTER SAUCE AND VEGETARIAN OYSTER SAUCE

A thick, dark brown sauce made from oysters. It doesn't have much of a fishy flavour, more umami and savouriness. Used throughout East Asia, it brings a depth to dishes that cannot be replaced. From stir-fried noodles to soup and stews, it's an essential. There are many vegetarian oyster sauces on the market that are mushroom based, which work perfectly too!

SALT

TABLE SALT: Refined salt is used throughout kitchens across the world, and it's fairly forgiving if you accidentally use too much. This is what I use as standard, and it's perfect for anything from soups and stews to noodles.

FLAKY SEA SALT: This is ideal for finishing a dish, for example on steaks, fish or potatoes.

SUGAR

WHITE GRANULATED SUGAR: Included in a lot of East Asian dishes, this is the most commonly used sugar in this book – not for sweetening dishes but rather to balance the salty and savoury notes and round out the recipe as a whole.

ROCK SUGAR: Less sweet and more mellow, rock sugar has a rounded and deep flavour. It's often used for in recipes that call for braising, like poached chicken or slow-cooked meats. It provides a complex flavour profile, rather than just added sweetness.

UDON NOODLES

I love udon noodles – to me, there is no better noodle. They're chewy, satisfying and just delicious. So don't be surprised to find a fair few udon recipes in this book . . .

FROZEN UDON: Frozen noodles are usually just fresh noodles that have been frozen. If you can get your hands on these, you're winning. They're close to restaurant-quality noodles, which have a better texture and quick cooking time. There's no need for the water to rehydrate them as they're already cooked, just add them to boiled water and once they're defrosted and loose, they're ready.

INSTANT FRESH UDON: My second go-to if I can't get my hands on frozen udon. Like the frozen udon, they're already cooked and there's no need to rehydrate them like pasta or instant ramen. Add them to boiled water and, once they're loose, they're ready. It's hard to overcook these, and they still have a great texture.

DRIED UDON: Still a great option, but these are dehydrated so cooking time is key. Like pasta, al dente udon is the best for texture and chew. Cook for 1 minute less than the time stated on the packet to retain their chew.

VINEGARS

RICE VINEGAR: The most common vinegar used in East Asian cuisine, it's distilled until white and clear. It's typically mild in flavour and its purpose is mainly to add a sour or tangy dimension to dishes. Used in salad dressings or noodle soups.

CHINESE BLACK VINEGAR: Think of this as the balsamic vinegar of the East. It's aged for years until funky and dark in colour, with nutty notes. Perfect for smashed cucumbers, sauces and dumplings.

APPLE CIDER VINEGAR: A sweet and slightly cloudy vinegar that can be used to replace either of the above, and is widely used in Korean cooking to balance the spiciness of dishes.

RICE (AND HOW TO COOK IT)

There's nothing that says home to me more than stepping through the front door and getting a whiff of freshly steamed rice. Whether or not rice is cooked well can, in my opinion, make or break a dish. So here's a little explainer on the key types I use and the different ways of cooking them.

Rice comes in all sizes and colours. You might be familiar with the most common: white and brown. They're all the same grain, with white having the outside shell removed, hence the 'healthier, more fibrous' label attached to brown rice (although personally, I find it harder to digest, but each to their own!). The shorter, fatter and chubbier the grain, the longer it takes to rehydrate, so these shorter grains usually benefit from soaking in cold water for 30 minutes (longer or shorter depending on the room temperature). In summer, 30 minutes is more than enough, whereas in winter, it may need a little longer. This ensures a fluffy, perfectly cooked grain of rice all the way into the middle. These short grains also require less water when steaming (see overleaf). Longer grains like Jasmine rice don't need soaking. They require more water and a slightly different method of cooking. One rule I stand by (religiously) is that you should never, ever boil and drain rice. Steaming it in a pan is the method used for centuries, so if it ain't broke – DON'T FIX IT. Plus, boiling and draining is more effort, so in the spirit of this book, why not sit back, relax and make it easy for yourself! The last rule is to never take the lid off a pan of rice until it's done, otherwise you release all the steam and mess the whole damn thing up!

Of course, this is all subjective. I'm a major rice nerd, but to some, rice is just rice, so . . . whatever floats your boat! Also – if you have a rice cooker, by all means use it (I love my one). They are great time-savers, and the result is just the same as cooking in a pan.

JASMINE RICE

The most commonly eaten rice throughout East and Southeast Asia, jasmine rice is named after the aroma it releases when cooked – there really is nothing like it. People in the West might know this as 'sticky rice', but that's something entirely different in the East (which I won't get into).

METHOD: Wash the rice in a bowl of water, then drain and repeat three times until the water runs clear. This is an essential step that helps to remove excess starch (much like soaking potatoes).

Once the rice is washed, drain it and place in a saucepan. Add water at a ratio of 1 part rice to 1.5 parts water. So, for 150g rice, you'd use 225ml water.

Cover and turn the heat to high, bringing the water to the boil. Once boiling, reduce the heat to the lowest setting and set a timer for 18 minutes. Do not open the lid or stir at any point. Once cooked, remove from the heat and set aside until needed. It's that simple.

JAPANESE SHORT-GRAIN RICE

More prevalent in East Asia (China, Japan, Korea and Taiwan), this is my favourite rice – it's something about its texture, taste and the way it soaks up sauce. It's the stickier of the two and takes a little more effort, but boy oh boy is it worth it.

METHOD: Wash the rice in a bowl of water, then drain and repeat three times until the water runs clear.

Once the rice is washed, drain it and place in a saucepan. Add water at a ratio of 1 part rice to 1.2 parts water. So, for 150g rice, you'd use 180ml water. Patience is a virtue now. Leave the rice to soak in the pan with the lid on for 30 minutes.

After 30 minutes, turn the heat to high and bring to the boil. Once boiling, reduce the heat to the lowest setting and cook for 11 minutes, remove the pan from the heat and set the timer for 10 minutes. This is a fail-safe method I've been using for years, and in my opinion, it's the easiest.

PORTIONS AND SUBSTITUTIONS

Rice is served with dishes throughout this book, and in most cases, how much you serve is up to you. I recommend about 150–200g cooked rice per person. Generally, 150g of uncooked rice will yield 300g of cooked rice. If using a rice cooker, 1 cup of uncooked rice will yield 2 portions of cooked rice.

If you can't get or don't have the rice suggested in a recipe, it can always be substituted for a type you already have.

Substitutions for jasmine rice are (in order): Japanese short-grain, Japanese medium-grain, basmati.

Substitutions for Japanese short-grain are (in order): Japanese medium-grain, jasmine, basmati.

JUST WOKEN UP?

BREAKFAST & BRUNCH

Whether I wake up in a good or bad mood is incredibly unpredictable for me, but my first thought isn't what I'm going to wear, do or see – it's what I'm going to eat (especially if those stomach grumbles are the thing putting me in a bad mood . . . it do be like that!). My mind doesn't usually function without food or spice, so breakfast is especially important to kill the grog. Expect everything from eggs and pancakes to rice and noodles. Whether you have a little or a lot of time to spare, these will help you to prepare for the inevitable 'long day'!

SPRING ONION PANCAKES WITH CURRY SAUCE v

A clash of titans! If Malaysian breakfast came up against Chinese breakfast, this would be the result. Here we have a wonderfully crispy, buttery pancake served with a quick curry sauce to dip it in. There are a lot of spring onions involved – some soft and some crispy and burnt.

125g plain flour
100ml boiling water
¼ tsp salt
½ tsp MSG
½ tsp granulated sugar
3 spring onions, thinly sliced
small bunch of coriander, thinly sliced
small bunch of chives, thinly sliced
1 tbsp sesame oil
1 tbsp vegetable oil, plus extra for frying
1 tbsp sesame seeds
2 medium eggs
2 tbsp unsalted butter

For the curry sauce
1 tbsp red curry paste
400ml coconut milk
1 tsp granulated sugar

Combine the flour, boiling water, salt, MSG and sugar in a bowl using chopsticks. Stir until a slightly sticky dough has formed, then use your hands to knead it in the bowl for 8–10 minutes, or until the dough becomes soft and malleable. Wrap tightly in cling film and set aside to rest at room temperature for 15 minutes.

Put the spring onions, coriander and chives into a bowl and toss to combine.

Next, make the curry sauce. Put the curry paste, coconut milk and sugar into a saucepan over a high heat and bring to the boil. Whisk to combine, then continue to cook for 5 minutes, or until reduced by a third. Pour into a small bowl and set aside.

In a small bowl, combine the sesame oil and vegetable oil.

Once the dough has rested, divide it into two equal portions. Roll each portion into a circle, around 2.5mm thick. Brush with the oil mixture, then sprinkle over half the spring onion, coriander and chive mixture, followed by half the sesame seeds. Roll the dough into a cigar shape, then roll that into a spiral, like a snail shell. Repeat with the remaining portion of dough, then gently roll out the spirals of dough to form pancakes no more than 5mm thick.

Heat a frying pan over medium heat for about 1 minute, then add a knob of the butter and a splash of oil. Fry one of the pancakes for 2–3 minutes on each side until golden and crisp, then remove from the pan. Add another splash of oil to the pan and crack in an egg. Using chopsticks, break the yolk and marble it into the white. Place the cooked pancake on top of the egg and cook for 1 minute. Repeat for the remaining pancake.

Cut the pancakes into quarters and serve with the curry sauce on the side. Dip into the sauce to eat.

GREEN EGGS AND RICE

Crispy fried eggs doused in the tangiest herby sauce (which is made in minutes) on top of piping hot white rice is one of my household breakfast staples. Inspired by my travels in Thailand and the crispy fried eggs with runny yolks I ate there, this is a marriage made in heaven.

6 tbsp vegetable oil
3 medium eggs
½ small bunch of coriander, roughly chopped
½ small bunch of mint, roughly chopped
½ small bunch of Thai basil, roughly chopped
2 tbsp shop-bought fried shallots
cooked jasmine rice (see page 23), to serve

For the herby green sauce
2 garlic cloves
1 bird's eye chilli
½ small bunch of coriander
½ small bunch of mint
½ small bunch of Thai basil
1 tbsp fish sauce
1 tbsp granulated sugar
juice of 2 limes

Put all the ingredients for the sauce into a small food processor and blend for 30–60 seconds until smooth. Pour into a bowl and set aside.

Heat the vegetable oil in a frying pan over a high heat for about 2 minutes. Grab two small bowls and separate one of the eggs. Once the oil is shimmering hot and just shy of smoking, add the egg white to the oil and cook for 1 minute, being careful of spitting. Once the egg white has turned slightly brown and crispy on the edges, gently place the egg yolk in the middle of the white, then use a spoon to baste the egg with the oil from the pan and cook for a further 30 seconds. This trick ensures a crispy egg white and runny yolk. Remove the egg from the pan and repeat with the remaining two.

Put the freshly cooked rice onto a plate, top with the crispy fried eggs and generously pour the herby green sauce on top. Garnish with a handful of the roughly chopped herbs and sprinkle with plenty of fried shallots.

SWEET SOY SCRAMBLED EGGS

Creamy, buttery, well-seasoned scrambled eggs on toast, drizzled with a sticky sweet spring onion soy sauce and topped with lashings of Parmesan! Unlike the Western low-and-slow method of making scrambled eggs, this is the faster, more furious Asian style. Cooked in a scorching hot pan and ribboned to perfection, timing is key here as it cooks in seconds! Omit the ham for a vegetarian-friendly version or get creative and add in whatever you'd like!

3 medium eggs
1 slice of cooked ham, diced
small bunch of chives, thinly sliced
1 tsp granulated sugar
pinch of salt
pinch of MSG
pinch of ground white pepper (or black pepper)
1 tsp sesame oil
½ tsp cornflour mixed with ½ tbsp water
1 tbsp dark soy sauce
1 tsp light soy sauce
1 spring onion, cut into thirds
3 tsp vegetable oil
1 slice of sourdough bread
2 tbsp unsalted butter

Crack the eggs into a bowl, then add the ham, chives, sugar, salt, MSG, white pepper and sesame oil. Pour the cornstarch slurry into the eggs and beat for about 2 minutes to combine thoroughly, then set aside.

In a separate bowl, combine the dark and light soy sauce. Stir to combine.

Put the spring onion and 2 teaspoons of the vegetable oil into a small frying pan over a medium heat and cook for 2–3 minutes, or until the spring onions have browned. Remove from the heat and discard the spring onions. Pour the soy sauce mixture into the pan and swirl to combine, then pour into a bowl.

Toast the bread, then spread with half the butter and place on a plate.

Heat the remaining butter and vegetable oil in a frying pan over a high heat for about 2 minutes, or until the butter begins to vigorously bubble. Pour the eggs into the pan. Use a spatula to push the eggs from one side to the other, creating ribbons. Tilt the pan to cover the pan with more egg. Repeat the process 3–4 times, or until eggs are cooked to your liking – I prefer mine to be slightly runny on top.

Drape the eggs over the toast and drizzle with the sweet soy.

TRIPLE-THREAT SPRING ONION NOODLES v

PREP TIME 5 MINUTES
SERVES 2
COOK TIME 10 MINUTES

The secret to these noods lies in the sauce! A mixture of shallot, spring onion and chilli, slowly cooked until jammy and then seasoned with the Chinese trio of salt, sugar and MSG. It's incredibly addictive. Simplicity is key and these noodles prove it: minimal ingredients but an explosion of flavour! Pair with any type of noodles (preferably one with a chewy texture – udon or egg noodles also work great) and add a crispy fried egg on top if you'd like!

2 spring onions
1 shallot, halved
1 bird's eye chilli, or to taste
4 tbsp vegetable oil
1 tsp salt
1 tsp granulated sugar
1 tsp MSG
1 vegetarian oyster sauce (or oyster sauce)
1 tbsp sesame oil
1 tsp sesame seeds
3 packets of instant noodles (any type)
small bunch of coriander, roughly sliced
1 tbsp light soy sauce
1 tsp dark soy sauce

Put the spring onions, shallot and chilli into a food processor and blend until fine. Alternatively, chop with a knife.

Heat the oil in a small frying pan over a medium-high heat for 1 minute, then add the blended onion mixture, lower the heat to medium-low and fry for 5 minutes, stirring occasionally, until golden brown. Remove from the heat and add the salt, sugar, MSG, oyster sauce, sesame oil and sesame seeds. Stir well to combine. Set aside.

Bring a saucepan of water to the boil and cook the noodles (without adding the flavouring sachets) for 1 minute less than the time stated on the packet, then drain and place back in the pan.

Add the coriander and light and dark soy sauces and stir well to coat the noodles. Pour the spring onion oil into the noodles and stir well again, then plate up and enjoy!

PEANUT BUTTER BACON FRENCH TOAST

PREP TIME 5 MINUTES
SERVES 1
COOK TIME 10 MINUTES

This is a twist on my favourite Cantonese breakfast classic, Hong Kong-style French toast, which is eaten by many thousands of people every morning in Hong Kong. It's one of the most decadent breakfasts and a perfect way to start the day. It's gooey, luxurious and seriously addictive. My version takes it to the next level, adding cheese, bacon, peanut butter, chilli oil and Japanese mayonnaise! While this might sound like a crazy combo, trust me, it's elite.

100ml vegetable oil
3 rashers of streaky bacon
2 tbsp smooth peanut butter
3 slices of brioche or soft white bread
2 slices of American cheese
2 medium eggs
¼ tsp salt
small bunch of chives, very thinly sliced
knob of unsalted butter
1 tbsp Japanese mayonnaise, such as Kewpie

Put a splash of oil and the bacon into a cold frying pan over a medium heat and fry for 3–5 minutes until crispy, then remove and slice thinly.

Spread the peanut butter on two of the slices of bread, from edge to edge. Place a slice of cheese on each piece of bread and sprinkle over the bacon pieces. Stack one slice on top of the other, peanut butter and cheese side up. Place the remaining plain slice of bread on top to close the sandwich. Cut the crusts off the bread using a bread knife to create a square sandwich.

Heat the remaining oil in a small frying pan over a medium heat.

Beat the eggs with the salt in a shallow bowl until well combined, then place the sandwich into the eggs, starting with the sides and holding each side in the eggs for 5 seconds.

Place the sandwich into the hot oil, edge first. Hold for 10 seconds, then repeat for all edges. Once all the edges are sealed, cook for 2 minutes on each side, or until golden brown. Remove from the oil, place on a plate and sprinkle with the chives. Add a knob of butter on top and a spoonful of mayonnaise to the side.

FISH FINGER SANDO WITH LIME, WASABI AND CHIVE MAYO

Let's be real – nobody has time to make their own fish fingers after a long day! And ready-made options are becoming better and bougier. Freezer fish fingers? They're a 'hack' that's not really a 'hack' . . . we're just adding a little flair! Bang them in the oven and the hard part is over. A tangy, saucy, indulgent delight that's put together in the time it takes to cook the fish fingers. It's not just yummy, it's a stunner too!

4 frozen fish fingers
¼ red onion, thinly sliced
3 tbsp mayo (preferably Kewpie)
1 tsp wasabi paste
1 tsp soy sauce
handful of finely chopped chives
zest of 1 lime plus a squeeze of the juice
1 tbsp salted butter
2 slices of brioche
1 slice of American cheese

Preheat the oven to 240°C/220°C fan/gas mark 9.

Put the fish fingers onto a baking tray and cook in the oven according to the packet instructions.

Fill a bowl with cold water and soak the onion for 2 minutes, then drain.

Combine the mayonnaise, wasabi, soy sauce, chives, lime zest and juice in a bowl.

Heat the butter in a frying pan over a medium heat, then add the brioche and cook for 1–2 minutes, pressing down gently and occasionally moving it around the pan to ensure even toasting. Once golden, flip and repeat on the other side.

Place one slice of the brioche on a plate and generously dollop on the sauce, spreading it out evenly. Add the fish fingers, followed by the red onion. Lastly, add the American cheese and the second piece of bread.

Gently press down, then slice straight down the middle to serve.

CREAMY GOCHUJANG PRAWN NOODLES

PREP TIME 3 MINUTES
SERVES 1
COOK TIME 15 MINUTES

Saucy noodle-lovers HEAVEN! Prawns, spice and cream are not your usual go-to when you think of instant noodles, but keep reading. Think of it as a spicy seafood Asian alfredo! The deep notes from the gochujang bring the umami and spice, while the cream and mascarpone tame the heat. Cooked in minutes, it's an impressive dish that's hard to get wrong. Generous shavings of Parmesan and heaps of chives bring the dish to life – don't hold back!

2 tbsp olive oil
2 big garlic cloves, sliced
1 tbsp gochujang paste
1 tsp granulated sugar
50ml double cream
75g raw peeled king prawns (about 7)
1 tbsp mascarpone
1 packet of instant noodles (any type)
handful of finely chopped chives
handful of grated Parmesan

Heat a frying pan over a medium heat, then add the olive oil and garlic and fry for 1 minute until the garlic is soft but not coloured. Add the gochujang and sugar and stir to infuse them into the oil, breaking the paste up with your spoon or spatula until it gives off a reddish hue. Add the double cream and stir to create a smooth paste with no lumps, then add the king prawns and mascarpone. Cook for a further 2 minutes, or until the prawns turn pink. Remove from the heat.

Bring a saucepan of water to the boil and cook the noodles for 1 minute less than the time stated on the packet (without adding the flavouring sachets), then drain, reserving 5 tablespoons of the cooking water.

Place the frying pan with the prawns back over a medium heat and add the noodles, chives and reserved cooking water. Mix for 1 minute to coat the noodles with the sauce.

Transfer the noodles to a plate and shake the plate slightly to spread out the noodles, then sprinkle a generous amount of Parmesan on top.

DUMPLING SOUP NOODLES

Combining the two best things to come from Chinese cuisine – dumplings and noodles – this is a spicy, savoury and rich soup that will give you a quick fix for all your cravings. Nobody has time to make their own dumplings, and if you do then you certainly didn't have a long day (I'm very jealous)! Tip: boil the dumplings in a separate pot of water to keep the broth fresh.

1 tbsp vegetable oil
1 banana shallot, finely chopped
1 garlic clove, finely chopped
1 tbsp red curry paste
400ml coconut milk
200ml chicken stock
1 tsp fish sauce
1 pak choi, trimmed and leaves separated
6 frozen dumplings (choose your favourite brand)
2 x 200g packets of frozen (or fresh) udon noodles
1 spring onion, thinly sliced
1 tbsp sesame seeds
small bunch of coriander, thinly sliced
small bunch of mint, thinly sliced
1 tsp chilli oil
1 lime, cut into wedges

Put a saucepan over a high heat for about 1 minute, then add the vegetable oil, shallot and garlic. Gently fry for 1–2 minutes, being careful not to let the garlic burn. Stir in the curry paste and allow to cook out for a minute, then pour in the coconut milk, chicken stock and fish sauce. Bring to the boil, cook for 3 minutes, then lower the heat and keep warm.

Meanwhile, bring a saucepan of water to the boil and blanch the pak choi leaves for 1 minute. Remove and set aside. Add the dumplings to the water and cook according to the packet instructions, then remove and set aside. Finally, add the noodles and cook for about 3 minutes, then drain.

Divide the noodles between bowls, then add the dumplings and pak choi on top. Ladle in the soup until the top of the noodles are covered. Sprinkle with spring onion and sesame seeds and the coriander and mint. Drizzle with your favourite chilli oil and garnish with a wedge of lime.

TIP Thicker-skinned dumplings made for boiling, such as wontons, work perfectly here, but other dumplings like gyoza would also work well.

CREAMY BAKED PRAWN RICE

PREP TIME 5 MINUTES · SERVES 1 · COOK TIME 20 MINUTES

During my travels in Tokyo I came across a baked rice dish made with béchamel sauce and seafood, called Doria. It came out bubbling hot with a ton of cheese and pools of sauce. It didn't seem typically Japanese at all. Intrigued, I did my research and soon realised that Japanese people have an obsession with all things gratin – and so do I! Let it rest though, or you might burn your tongue.

1½ tbsp unsalted butter, plus extra for greasing
½ onion, diced
2–3 florets broccoli, diced
200g cooked Japanese short-grain rice (see page 23)
4 tsp light soy sauce
1 tbsp olive oil
2 garlic cloves, sliced
2 rashers of streaky bacon, sliced
70g raw or cooked peeled king prawns, sliced
75ml white wine
240ml milk
1 tbsp plain flour
50g Gruyère (or Cheddar), grated
1 tbsp panko breadcrumbs
10g Parmesan, grated
small bunch of chives, thinly sliced
salt and freshly ground black pepper

Grease a small, deep oven dish with butter.

Heat ½ tablespoon of the butter in a frying pan over a medium-high heat, then fry the onion and broccoli for 3–4 minutes. Add the rice and use a wooden spoon to gently separate the grains. Season with a generous pinch of salt, black pepper and half the soy sauce. Mix to combine well. Transfer the rice to the prepared oven dish and cover with a damp tea towel to stop it drying out. Set aside.

Pour the olive oil into same pan, then fry the garlic, bacon and prawns over a medium heat for 2–3 minutes until the bacon has cooked but not coloured. Add the white wine and cook for a further 1 minute until the alcohol has burnt off. Transfer the mixture to a bowl and set aside.

Heat the milk in a microwave or small pan until warmed.

Melt the remaining tablespoon of butter in a small saucepan over a medium-low heat, then add the flour and stir for 1–2 minutes until smooth. Gradually pour in the milk while stirring. Mix well to combine before pouring in more milk. Once all the milk has been incorporated, add a generous pinch of salt, 1 teaspoon of black pepper and the remaining soy sauce. Reduce the heat to low and cook for 1–2 minutes while stirring. Add the bacon and prawn mixture, including any liquid in the bowl, then mix well and pour on top of the rice. Sprinkle over the Gruyère followed by the panko breadcrumbs.

Preheat your grill to maximum heat, then place the rice on a high shelf under the grill and cook for 5 minutes, or until the cheese is golden and bubbling.

Remove from the oven, then sprinkle with the Parmesan and chives before serving.

HK-STYLE BREAKFAST BAP

PREP TIME 5 MINUTES
SERVES 2
COOK TIME 10 MINUTES

In East Asia, and particularly Hong Kong, Spam is widely eaten for breakfast with noodles, in fried rice and in sandwiches. Think of it as the cousin of bacon – if you like bacon, you'll like this. It's a salty, savoury and flavourful fuss-free alternative that can be found in any supermarket. Fry it up, then glaze it with a sweet, sticky sauce and whack it in whatever!

small bunch of chives, thinly sliced
2 tbsp mayonnaise
2 tbsp sriracha (or your favourite hot sauce)
2 tbsp light soy sauce
1 tbsp mirin
1 tbsp sake (or water)
1 tbsp light brown soft sugar
200g tin of Spam, sliced lengthways into 4 pieces
2 tbsp unsalted butter
2 brioche burger buns, sliced in half
2 tbsp vegetable oil
2 medium eggs
pinch of salt
2 slices of American cheese

Put the chives, mayonnaise and sriracha into a bowl and stir to combine, then set aside.

In a separate bowl, combine the soy sauce, mirin, sake and brown sugar and stir until the sugar has dissolved.

Heat a dry frying pan over a medium-high heat for about 1 minute. Add the butter to the pan, followed by the buns, cut side down. Toast for 1–2 minutes until golden, then remove from the pan and set aside.

Pour the oil into the same pan, then crack in the eggs, season with the salt and fry sunny side up for about 2 minutes, keeping the yolk runny. Remove the eggs from the pan and set aside.

Add the Spam slices to the same pan and fry for 1–2 minutes on each side, or until golden. Pour in the soy sauce mixture and gently shake the pan. The sauce will slowly thicken into a glaze. Flip the Spam slices to glaze them on all sides.

Assemble the burgers: place two slices of Spam on the bottom of each bun, followed by a slice of cheese. Add the fried eggs and a generous amount of the spicy mayonnaise. Add the top of the brioche bun and enjoy!

BANGERS AND TOMATO RICE

This one-pot tomato rice dish is topped with crispy bite-sized pieces of sausage, toasted rice and shallots cooked in the rendered sausage fat. It's a flavourful but simple meal that pays homage to the classic English breakfast, but with Cantonese street-food influences and an addictive sweet and salty soy sauce that is drizzled on top.

200g jasmine rice
3 British pork sausages
2 tbsp vegetable oil
2 rashers of streaky bacon, chopped into 1cm pieces
2 banana shallots, thinly sliced
1 garlic clove, very finely chopped
1 tsp tomato purée
1 tbsp sriracha
1 large tomato, diced
200ml water
1 tbsp dark soy sauce
1 tbsp light soy sauce
1 tsp oyster sauce
1 tsp granulated sugar
1 tsp sesame oil
1 spring onion, thinly sliced
2 tbsp sesame seeds
small bunch of chives, thinly sliced
1 tbsp chilli oil
freshly ground black pepper

Put the rice into a bowl and cover with cold water. Rinse the rice and then pour out the water. Repeat this twice, or until the water is clear, then drain.

Squeeze the meat out of the sausage casings and then form into small meatballs and set aside.

Heat 1 tablespoon of the vegetable oil in a lidded saucepan over a medium heat for 1 minute, then add the sausage meatballs to the pan and fry for 3–5 minutes until golden and crisp, stirring occasionally. Once golden, remove from the pan onto a plate and set aside.

Add the remaining oil to the pan along with the sliced bacon and shallots and fry for 2 minutes, or until slightly golden and crispy, then add the garlic and fry for 30 seconds. Add the tomato purée and sriracha and cook for a further 30 seconds, or until the oil turns a reddish hue. Add the drained rice and diced tomato and stir a minute. Add a few cracks of black pepper and then pour in the water, give it a stir and turn the heat to high. Put the lid on and bring to the boil. Once boiling, lower the heat to the lowest setting and cook for 18 minutes.

Meanwhile, combine the dark and light soy sauce, oyster sauce, sugar and sesame oil in a small bowl. Stir until the sugar has dissolved and then set aside.

Once the rice has cooked, remove it from the heat and add the spring onion and half the sesame seeds. Gently fold the rice using a wooden spoon, making sure not to break up the grains.

Spread the rice onto plates, then top with the crispy sausage, chives and the remaining sesame seeds. Drizzle with the sauce and some of your favourite chilli oil.

TIP Simply seasoned pork sausages work great in this, but you can use any type – caramelised onion sausages would work well.

PRAWN AND HERB SALAD

I crave this zingy prawn salad most mornings. It ticks every box: moreish, tangy and, most importantly, easy. The secret is the traditional Cantonese cooking technique of pouring hot oil over aromatics to scorch them and bring out their aroma – the food theatrics that come with it are just an added bonus. This pairs well with a steaming bowl of white rice or is even a great filling for a sandwich!

2cm piece of fresh ginger, finely grated
zest and juice of 1 lime
juice of 1 lemon
1 tbsp light soy sauce
1 tsp sesame oil
pinch of MSG
1 tsp mayonnaise
1 tbsp hoisin sauce
3 spring onions
½ red onion, very thinly sliced
3 tbsp vegetable oil
250g asparagus, woody ends snapped off
200g cooked peeled king prawns, halved lengthways
½ cucumber, deseeded and sliced diagonally into thin strips
1 celery stick, sliced diagonally
large bunch of coriander, roughly chopped
small bunch of mint, roughly chopped
small bunch of chives, roughly chopped
1 red chilli, deseeded and cut into thin matchsticks
1 tbsp sesame seeds
1 tbsp shop-bought fried shallots
1 tbsp chilli oil

Combine the ginger, lime zest and juice, lemon juice, soy sauce, sesame oil, MSG, mayonnaise and hoisin sauce in a small bowl and stir well, then set aside. This is your dressing.

Cut the spring onions into thirds, then thinly slice each third vertically into strips. Put the spring onions and sliced red onion to a bowl of ice-cold water.

Heat 1 tablespoon of the oil in a frying pan over a high heat for 1 minute, then add the asparagus and cook for 2 minutes, occasionally shaking the pan to cook them evenly. Remove from the pan and leave to cool, then slice into thirds diagonally.

Drain the red onion and spring onions.

Pour the salad dressing into a large bowl and add the prawns, followed by the cucumber, celery, red onion and asparagus. Add the herbs, spring onions and chilli, then sprinkle the sesame seeds on top.

Heat the remaining oil in a small saucepan over a high heat for around 2 minutes until the oil is shimmering and just shy of smoking. Gently pour the hot oil on top of the spring onions and chilli and watch it crackle and pop!

Toss the salad, making sure to pick up all the dressing from the bottom of the bowl. Mix until the dressing has thoroughly coated the salad.

Transfer to a plate and sprinkle over the fried shallots, then drizzle with your favourite chilli oil.

MARBLED EGGS AND CHICKEN OVER RICE

PREP TIME 10 MINUTES
SERVES 1
COOK TIME 10 MINUTES

This chicken and egg rice bowl is inspired by the Japanese dish oyakodon (literally 'parent and child bowl'), which I ate during my trip to Japan and which totally won my heart. A twist on this soul-warming Japanese classic, my version includes a rich and spicy garlic butter poured on top. If you have dashi powder, use it!

2 tbsp light soy sauce
2 tbsp mirin
½ tsp granulated sugar
5g sachet of dashi powder (optional)
75ml water
2 medium eggs
1 tbsp unsalted butter
2 garlic cloves, finely chopped
1 tsp chilli powder
1 tbsp vegetable oil
2 skinless and boneless chicken thighs, cut into bite-sized pieces
pinch of salt
handful of baby spinach leaves
½ white onion, sliced
1 sheet of nori seaweed (optional), cut into thin strips
bunch of chives, thinly sliced
1 tbsp sesame seeds
cooked Japanese short-grain rice (see page 23), to serve

Combine the soy sauce, mirin, sugar, dashi powder (if using) and water in a small bowl and stir until the sugar has dissolved.

Crack the eggs into a separate bowl and drag a pair of chopsticks through the eggs to marble the yolks with the whites, no more than a few times. Do not beat.

Put the butter, garlic and chilli powder into a small frying pan over a medium heat and cook for 1–2 minutes, or until the garlic is golden but not burnt. Pour into a small bowl and set aside.

Wipe out the frying pan and add the oil, then heat for about 1 minute over a medium-high heat. Lightly season the chicken with the salt, then add to the pan and fry for 1–2 minutes on each side until nicely coloured. Scatter the spinach and onion on top, then pour over the soy sauce mixture and cook for 2 minutes. Gently pour the marbled eggs into the pan, making sure to cover all areas. Cook for a further 1–2 minutes, or until the egg is cooked to your liking. I prefer the eggs to be slightly runny.

Put the rice into a bowl and sprinkle over the nori strips. Gently pour the contents of the pan on top, making sure to cover the entire bowl. Pour the garlic butter on top and generously sprinkle with the chives and sesame seeds.

NOTE Try adding a raw egg yolk on top for extra richness!

SESAME GINGER SALMON CLAYPOT RICE

Fish and rice for breakfast may seem odd, but in Japan it's probably the most common breakfast you'll see! What better way to get the day started than with a load of carbs and fish. Steamed white rice and perfectly flaky salmon with a rich ginger and sesame sauce over the top is a heavenly way to kick off your morning.

150g Japanese short-grain rice, washed
180ml water
120g skinless salmon fillet, thinly sliced
½ tsp salt
¼ tsp granulated sugar
¼ tsp MSG
¼ tsp ground white pepper
1 tsp water
½ tsp cornflour
1 tsp sesame oil
1 medium egg

For the ginger and sesame sauce
2cm piece of fresh ginger, finely chopped
1 small garlic clove, finely chopped
½ spring onion, finely chopped
1 tsp sesame seeds
few sprigs of coriander, thinly sliced
1 tbsp vegetable oil
1 tbsp light soy sauce
1 tsp dark soy sauce
1 tsp oyster sauce
¼ tsp salt
½ tsp MSG
½ tsp granulated sugar
1 tsp sesame oil
1 tsp water

Put the rice into a bowl with the water and set aside to soak.

Put the salmon into a bowl with the salt, sugar, MSG, white pepper, water and cornflour. Mix well, then set aside to marinate while you make the sauce.

Put the ginger, garlic, spring onion, sesame seeds and coriander into a small heatproof bowl. Heat the vegetable oil in a small pan over a high heat until almost smoking and pour into the bowl. Stir to combine. Add the remaining ingredients for the sauce and stir until the sugar has dissolved. Set aside.

Add the sesame oil to a claypot or small saucepan and swirl the pan to cover the base with oil. Add the rice and its soaking water. Cover and bring to the boil, then turn to the lowest heat and cook for 10 minutes.

After 10 minutes, arrange the salmon slices on the rice, spreading them out as much as possible. Put the lid back on and cook for 5 minutes, then crack the egg onto the salmon, cover again and cook for a further 3 minutes. Remove from the heat, drizzle over the sauce, cover and leave to rest for 5 minutes before eating.

NEED TO EAT NOW?

QUICK & EASY

Do you ever tell your mates a time to meet but you're still sitting at home at that exact time with no food in your belly? Well, not me! Don't be that guy, and don't be late! We all have those days when we don't have the drive, energy or time to whip up the good stuff. These recipes will show you how easy it is to rustle up a good meal in no time. Impressive, nourishing, but most importantly, banging!

MISO MUSHROOM UDON v

An easy but decadent creamy vegetarian udon, full of umami from the miso paste and topped with a gooey soft-boiled egg.

PREP TIME 7 MINUTES
SERVES 2
COOK TIME 15 MINUTES

2 medium eggs
2 x 250g packets of frozen (or fresh) udon noodles
2 tbsp olive oil
300g chestnut mushrooms, thinly sliced
3 garlic cloves, finely chopped
1 shallot, finely chopped
knob of unsalted butter
2 tbsp mirin
2 tbsp light soy sauce
150ml single cream
2 tbsp miso paste
4 tbsp sesame seeds, toasted
2 spring onions, thinly sliced

Bring a saucepan of water to the boil and gently add the eggs. Cook for 6 minutes, then transfer the eggs to a bowl of ice-cold water.

Put the noodles into the same pan of boiling water and cook for about 3 minutes until the noodles have separated, then drain and set aside.

Peel the eggs and slice in half, then set aside.

Heat a large frying pan over a medium-high heat for about 2 minutes, then add the oil. Add the mushrooms and fry for 5 minutes, stirring occasionally, until they're a nice golden colour. Add the garlic, shallots and butter and fry for a further 1 minute. Add the mirin, soy sauce, cream and miso paste and stir to incorporate. Add the noodles and stir for 30 seconds. If the sauce is too dry, add a tablespoon of water.

Transfer the noodles to plates and cover with the sesame seeds, then top with the spring onions and add the soft-boiled eggs.

TIP Toast the sesame seeds and slightly crush them in a pestle and mortar. You can also add grated Parmesan to make it even more indulgent!

FIVE-MINUTE CHILLI OIL UDON WITH CUCUMBER AND CORIANDER v

This is like the noodle equivalent of the Big Mac. Super-simple, sweet, saucy and with layers of flavour, it's dangerously addictive! To keep it as saucy as possible, everything is made in one bowl, so not a single drop is lost. There's a touch of food theatre, too, as you watch the hot oil scorch and sizzle the garlic and chilli powder to make the glossy sauce for the noodles.

PREP TIME 2 MINUTES
SERVES 1
COOK TIME 5 MINUTES

- 1 tsp ground Sichuan peppercorns
- 1 tsp chilli powder
- 1 tsp sesame seeds
- 1 garlic clove, finely chopped
- 1 tbsp very finely chopped spring onion
- 1 tbsp vegetable oil
- 1 tbsp light soy sauce
- 1 tsp dark soy sauce
- 1 tsp vegetarian oyster sauce (or oyster sauce)
- 1 tsp Chinese black vinegar (or balsamic vinegar)
- 1 tsp granulated sugar
- pinch of MSG (optional)
- 200g packet of fresh (or frozen) udon noodles
- 4 slices of cucumber, cut into matchsticks
- handful of coriander (leaves and stalks), roughly chopped

Put the ground Sichuan peppercorns, chilli powder, sesame seeds, garlic and spring onion into a serving bowl.

Heat the vegetable oil in a small saucepan over a high heat for about 3 minutes until smoking, then carefully pour the hot oil onto the ingredients in the serving bowl and give it a stir. Add the light soy sauce, dark soy sauce, oyster sauce, black vinegar, sugar and MSG and stir until the sugar has dissolved.

Bring a saucepan of water to the boil and cook the noodles for 3 minutes, gently loosening the noodles while they cook. Drain the noodles and add them directly to the serving bowl. Give it a good mix, making sure the sauce completely coats the noodles. Add the cucumber and coriander and give it one more thorough mix. Give the noodles a big slurp and enjoy!

SHIITAKE MUSHROOM AND CORIANDER EGG DROP SOUP v

PLUS SOAKING TIME

One of my favourite things is the classic egg drop soups found in Chinese takeaways. Having grown up in one, I can safely say I've probably eaten over a thousand in my lifetime! There are so many variations for different moods, but this one is an ode to my favourite. Meaty mushrooms, silky egg and the best herb of all time, coriander *mic drop*. A drizzle of vinegar and you're in heaven.

3 pieces of dried wood ear mushroom, sliced (optional)
2 medium eggs
1 tsp salt, plus extra for the eggs
800ml beef or vegetable stock
60g shiitake mushrooms, finely chopped
150g silken tofu, cut into cubes
1 thumb-sized piece of fresh ginger, very finely chopped
small bunch of coriander, roughly chopped
1 tsp MSG
1 tsp light soy sauce
1 tsp granulated sugar
1 tsp ground white pepper
3 tbsp cornflour mixed with 3 tbsp water, or as needed
1 tbsp sesame oil
1 tbsp Chinese red vinegar (optional)

If using, put the dried wood ear mushrooms into a bowl and cover with boiling water. Set aside to soak for 30 minutes.

Meanwhile, crack the eggs into a bowl, add a pinch of salt and beat with a fork.

Pour the beef stock into a saucepan over a high heat and bring to the boil. Once boiling, add the shiitake mushrooms, rehydrated wood ear mushrooms, tofu, ginger and coriander. Cook for 1 minute, then add the salt, MSG, light soy sauce, sugar and white pepper. Cook for a further 1–2 minutes, then reduce the heat to the lowest setting. While stirring the soup with a spoon or chopsticks, slowly pour in the cornflour slurry. It will gradually thicken the soup. If it's too thin, add more slurry; if too thick, add a splash of cold water.

Next, slowly pour in the beaten egg while stirring. Turn the heat back up to high and cook for 45 seconds. Remove from the heat.

Ladle the soup into bowls, then drizzle over the sesame oil and vinegar. Mix it up and enjoy.

SPICY GARLIC BUTTER UDON WITH SMASHED CUCUMBER v

PREP TIME 10 MINUTES
SERVES 2
COOK TIME 15 MINUTES

There's a love affair to be explored with spice and dairy, and this is the showcase for it! It's like the spicier, creamier Asian cousin of the carbonara. Paired with the tangiest smashed cucumber (that's right, you get to take your anger out on the cukes after a long day) and a perfectly boiled egg, it's slurpable down to the last drop. It might just be perfect.

2 medium eggs
2 x 250g packets of frozen (or fresh) udon noodles
1 tbsp salted butter
3 garlic cloves, very finely chopped
1 shallot, finely chopped
2 tbsp gochujang paste
200ml single cream
3 tbsp light soy sauce
40g Parmesan, grated
2 spring onions, thinly sliced

For the smashed cucumber
½ cucumber
1 garlic clove, very finely chopped
1 tsp chilli flakes
1 tbsp sesame seeds
2 tbsp apple cider vinegar (or any clear vinegar)
1 tsp granulated sugar
1 tbsp light soy sauce
1 tbsp sesame oil

Bring a saucepan of water to the boil and gently add the eggs. Cook for 6 minutes, then transfer the eggs to a bowl of ice-cold water.

Next make the smashed cucumber. Grab the cucumber and whack it with a rolling pin or the side of a cleaver. Cut it into 1cm slices, then transfer to a bowl. Add all the remaining ingredients, mix well and set aside.

Bring a saucepan of water to the boil and cook the noodles for 3 minutes, then drain and set aside.

Heat the butter in a large frying pan over a medium heat, then add the garlic and shallots and fry for 30 seconds. Add the gochujang and mix to combine for about 1 minute until the butter turns a reddish hue. Add the cream, soy sauce and Parmesan and cook for a further 2 minutes, stirring to combine.

Remove the pan from the heat, add the noodles and mix gently until the sauce has coated the noodles.

Transfer the noodles to shallow bowls. Peel the eggs and slice in half, then place on top of the noodles, followed by the smashed cucumber and finally a heap of spring onion. Enjoy!

BACON AND KIMCHI FRIED RICE, NORI, MAYO AND CHILLI BURNT CORN AND CRISPY FRIED EGG

A Korean BBQ staple but not your typical fried rice. It uses the same all-in-one pan technique, but this one's not the side dish, it's the main. It's fiery, salty and sweet. The corn is grilled whole on the cob, then mayonnaise is painted on to act as a glue for the chilli flakes and spring onion, just like on the streets of Mexico, blending two cuisines with an affection for spice. This dish is all in the prep – once you're ready, it comes together in no time at all.

1 sweetcorn cob
1 tbsp mayonnaise
1 tbsp chilli flakes
1 spring onion, very finely chopped
5 tbsp vegetable oil
1 large egg
1 tbsp unsalted butter
1 garlic clove, finely chopped
1 banana shallot, finely chopped
2 rashers of streaky bacon, sliced into 1cm pieces
3 tbsp kimchi
300g cooked Japanese short-grain rice (see page 23)
1 tbsp gochujang paste
1 tbsp sesame oil
1 tsp salt, plus extra for seasoning the egg
1 tsp granulated sugar
1 tbsp light soy sauce
1 tbsp sesame seeds
1 sheet of nori seaweed

Heat a dry frying pan over a high heat for around 3 minutes to get nice and hot. Add the sweetcorn and char for about 5 minutes, turning every minute, until almost burnt. Remove the corn from the pan and use a pastry brush or the back of a spoon to paint on the mayonnaise. Sprinkle on the chilli flakes and a third of the spring onion. Hold the corn upright and run a knife between the kernels and the cob. The kernels should stay stuck together and you should have big clusters of corn. Set aside.

Heat a frying pan over a high heat, then add the oil and fry the egg until the edges are brown and crisp. Season with salt and set aside.

Heat a wok or large frying pan over a high heat for 2 minutes, then add the butter, garlic, shallot and bacon. Gently stir-fry for 3 minutes, then add the kimchi and stir-fry for a further 2 minutes. Lower the heat to medium. Add the rice, gochujang, sesame oil, salt, sugar and soy sauce. Bash the rice with a spatula to separate the grains and stir until everything is combined, around 3 minutes. Add the sesame seeds and half the remaining spring onion, then use your hands to crush the nori into flakes straight into the rice.

Transfer the rice to a plate and add the chunks of burnt corn on top followed by the crispy fried egg and finally the remaining spring onion.

NEED TO EAT NOW? QUICK & EASY

CURRY EGG UDON v

Think katsu curry but minus the rice and with chewy, slurp-worthy udon noodles instead. The noodles are drenched in something between a soup and a sauce, drinkable but thick and rich, with marbled, silky eggs drizzled within!

1 tbsp vegetable oil
2 banana shallots, diced
1 thumb-sized piece of fresh ginger, grated
2 garlic cloves, very finely chopped
1 tbsp medium curry powder (or mild/hot, depending on your preference)
1 tsp chilli powder
½ tsp ground cumin
¼ tsp ground turmeric
400ml coconut milk
300ml vegetable or chicken stock
1 tbsp light soy sauce
1 tsp dark soy sauce
1 tsp light brown soft sugar
3 tbsp cornflour mixed with 3 tbsp water, or as needed
3 medium eggs, beaten
2 x 250g packets of frozen (or fresh) udon
small bunch of coriander, thinly sliced
2 spring onions, thinly sliced
1 tbsp sesame oil
1 tbsp chilli oil
salt and freshly ground black pepper

Heat the vegetable oil in a saucepan over a medium-high heat, then fry the shallots, ginger and garlic for 1–2 minutes. Add the curry powder, chilli powder, cumin and turmeric and fry for a minute, then pour in the coconut milk, chicken stock, light soy sauce and dark soy sauce along with the sugar and a pinch of salt and pepper. Stir to combine and then bring to the boil. Once boiling, reduce the heat to medium-low and cook for 6–8 minutes, or until reduced by a third.

Meanwhile, bring a saucepan of water to the boil and cook the noodles according to the packet instructions, then drain and divide between bowls.

Reduce the heat under the sauce to low and slowly pour in the cornflour slurry while stirring. It should be thick and glossy – if it's too thin, add more slurry.

In a circular motion, gently pour the beaten eggs into the curry. Use a pair of chopsticks to slowly drag them through the sauce in a figure of eight a few times. This will create silky ribbons of egg. Increase the heat to medium and cook for a further 1 minute.

Ladle the curry sauce on top of the noodles until fully covered. Finish with a handful of coriander and spring onion in the middle, then drizzle over the sesame oil and chilli oil.

GINGER CHILLI BEEF UDON

PREP TIME 10 MINUTES
SERVES 1
COOK TIME 10 MINUTES

Chewy fried udon and lashings of chilli, ginger and soy, finished with a squeeze of lime – a marriage made in heaven. This is a quick and easy stir-fried noodle dish that cooks in less than 10 minutes! The key to this dish is to prep everything before you start, as once the first ingredient hits the pan it's all systems go!

200g rib-eye steak, thinly sliced
½ tbsp light soy sauce
1 tsp sesame oil
250g packet of frozen (or fresh) udon noodles
3 tbsp vegetable oil
1 medium egg
1 thumb-sized piece of fresh ginger, very finely chopped
1 red chilli, thinly sliced
1 spring onion, quartered
½ red onion, sliced into 1cm pieces
handful of beansprouts
1 tbsp sesame seeds
small bunch of coriander, roughly chopped
1 lime wedge
1 tbsp chilli oil
salt and freshly ground black pepper

For the stir-fry sauce
½ tbsp light soy sauce
1 tsp fish sauce
1 tsp oyster sauce
1 tsp freshly ground black pepper
1 tsp dashi powder (optional)
2 tsp sesame oil
1 tsp granulated sugar

Put the steak into a bowl with a pinch of salt, the soy sauce, sesame oil and a few cracks of black pepper. Set aside.

In a separate bowl, combine all the ingredients for the stir-fry sauce.

Bring a saucepan of water to a boil and cook the noodles for about 3 minutes, then drain and set aside.

Heat the oil in a large frying pan over a high heat for 1–2 minutes, or until smoking. Crack the egg into the pan and flash-fry for 1–2 minutes until crispy around the edges but the yolk is still runny. Remove the egg and set aside. Add the steak to the pan and toss for 1–2 minutes, or until nicely browned. Remove the steak and set aside. Add the ginger, chilli, spring onion and red onion. Stir-fry for 30 seconds, then add the noodles. Cook for a further 1–2 minutes, then add the steak back to the pan along with the beansprouts. Pour the sauce around the edges of the pan and toss the noodles vigorously until fully coated in the sauce.

Transfer to a serving plate, then sprinkle over the sesame seeds, top with the crispy fried egg, a generous handful of coriander and finally a wedge of lime. Drizzle with your favourite chilli oil before serving.

CHICKEN THIGH AND HONEY GOCHUJANG INSTANT NOODLES

PREP TIME 5 MINUTES
SERVES 2
COOK TIME 15 MINUTES

Time to chuck away those salt-filled sachets that come with instant noodles. This is a spicy, saucy, home-made alternative that's miles better and just as quick to make. It hits every flavour profile you'd crave from East Asian cooking and is topped with the crispiest chicken and a chilli and onion salsa. You'll be making this weekly! No excuses!

2 skin-on boneless chicken thighs
2 packets of instant noodles (any type)
salt

For the chilli and onion salsa
½ red onion, diced
1 red chilli, sliced
1 green chilli, sliced
3 spring onions, sliced
1 garlic clove, crushed
4 tbsp light soy sauce
5 tbsp water
1 tbsp honey
2 tbsp sesame seeds

For the gochujang sauce
2 tbsp gochujang paste
1 tbsp gochugaru (Korean red pepper flakes; or use paprika)
1 tsp cayenne pepper
1 tbsp light soy sauce
1 tbsp clear honey
3 tbsp mirin
1 tbsp oyster sauce
1 tsp chicken stock powder
1 garlic clove, crushed
1 tbsp water
few cracks of black pepper

Dab the chicken with kitchen paper, then season both sides with salt and place into a cold frying pan, skin side down. Turn the heat to medium. Don't touch or move the chicken – this ensures the skin stays crispy and helps to render the fat. Cook for about 7 minutes, then flip and cook the other side for a further 3 minutes. Remove the chicken from the pan and set aside, and set the pan aside too (don't clean it out).

Combine all the ingredients for the chilli and onion salsa in a bowl and stir well until the honey has dissolved. Set aside.

In a separate bowl, combine all the ingredients for the gochujang sauce and mix well.

Bring a saucepan of water to the boil and cook the noodles for 1½ minutes less than the time stated on the packet (without adding the flavouring sachets), then drain, reserving 4 tablespoons of the cooking water.

Place the frying pan you used for the chicken over a medium heat and add the gochujang sauce. Fry for 1 minute, or until the sauce turns a darker red. Add the noodles and the reserved cooking water and stir until the sauce coats the noodles.

Transfer the noodles to a plate. Slice the chicken thighs and place on top of the noodles. Using a strainer or a spoon, strain the chilli and onion salsa, then sprinkle it on top.

SPICY CHICKEN ESCALOPE SANDO

If a Nashville rooster fell in love with a Sichuan hen, this is what it would look like. Shallow-fried chicken escalope dusted in a mixture of ground Sichuan peppercorns, chilli powder and cumin, sandwiched between two pieces of ciabatta and handfuls of coriander salad to cut through the spice. Split it in half and it serves two . . . which is not usually the case in my house!

1 tsp Sichuan peppercorns (or ground Sichuan pepper)
½ tsp cumin seeds (or ground cumin)
1 tbsp Chinese five-spice powder
1 skinless chicken breast
2 medium eggs
6 tbsp plain flour
6 tbsp panko breadcrumbs
200ml vegetable oil, or as needed
1 tbsp chilli powder
1 ciabatta (or any long loaf of bread), sliced in half
½ red onion, thinly sliced
¼ cucumber, thinly sliced
small bunch of coriander, roughly chopped
juice of ½ lime
2 tbsp Japanese mayonnaise, such as Kewpie (or regular mayo)
1 tbsp chilli oil (I like Lao Gan Ma)
2 slices of American cheese
salt

Put the Sichuan peppercorns and cumin seeds into a pestle and mortar and finely grind them, then add a big pinch of salt and the five-spice powder. Stir to combine.

Tear off a large sheet of baking paper (or cling film) and place the chicken breast on the left side, then fold the right side over the top. Using a meat tenderiser or rolling pin, bash the chicken to flatten it to 1–2cm thick. Generously sprinkle the spice mixture over both sides.

Crack the eggs into a bowl and vigorously beat with a fork, then pour onto a plate or small tray. Put the flour onto another plate or tray and season with a generous pinch of salt, then mix with a fork to incorporate. Pour the panko breadcrumbs onto a third plate. Line the plates up from left to right: flour, then egg and then breadcrumbs.

Place the chicken in the plate of flour and flip to cover both sides, making sure the flour has covered every part of the breast. Next, place the chicken in the beaten egg and flip to coat it completely. Finally, transfer the chicken to the breadcrumbs and flip again, ensuring every part of the breast is covered with breadcrumbs (press the breadcrumbs into the chicken with your fingers to make sure they are really stuck on).

Pour the vegetable oil into a large frying pan, ensuring the oil is about 1cm deep – you may need to add a bit more depending on the size of your pan. Heat the oil over a medium-high heat for 2–3 minutes, then gently place the breaded chicken into the oil. Cook for 2–3 minutes on each side, or until golden brown. While cooking, use a spoon to baste the hot oil over the chicken for an extra crispy finish. Remove the chicken from the pan and dust both sides with the chilli powder.

Discard the oil and place the pan back over a medium heat. Place the ciabatta in pan, cut side down, and toast for 1–2 minutes, or until golden brown. Remove and place on a plate or board.

Put the red onion, cucumber and coriander into a bowl, then add the lime juice and a pinch of salt. Mix to coat.

In a separate bowl, combine the mayonnaise and chilli oil and stir well.

Generously spread the chilli mayonnaise on the bottom of the ciabatta, then place the fried chicken on top, followed by the cheese. Add the coriander salad and finish with the top of the ciabatta. Cut in half and serve.

(See photo overleaf)

PARMESAN, HERB AND CHILLI BEEF SALAD

An earthy, fiery beef salad, with a ton of herbs and lashings of Parmesan, this is one for those summery days – a real crowd pleaser! Scorching a lemon in a dry pan gives it an amazing caramelised, jammy flavour, and when squeezed on top it brings everything together. Of course, the more Parmesan the better.

250g rib-eye steak
1 tbsp light soy sauce
1 tbsp freshly ground black pepper
pinch of flaky sea salt, plus extra to serve
1 lemon, halved
3 tbsp vegetable oil
1 tbsp unsalted butter
2 garlic cloves, smashed
¼ cucumber, peeled, deseeded and sliced diagonally
½ red onion, thinly sliced
small bunch of chives, roughly chopped
small bunch of basil, leaves picked
small bunch of mint, leaves picked
1 red chilli, thinly sliced
50g Parmesan, or to taste

For the dressing
1 tsp light soy sauce
2 tsp rice vinegar
1 tsp clear honey
2 tsp extra virgin olive oil
1 tsp sesame seeds

Season the steak on both sides with the sauce, black pepper and salt.

Heat a dry frying pan over a high heat for 2 minutes, or until smoking. Add the lemon, cut side down, and scorch for about 2 minutes. Don't touch the lemon while it is cooking, to allow it to caramelise. Once nicely burnt, remove from the pan and set aside.

Pour the oil into the hot pan, still set over a high heat, and swirl to coat. Add the steak and cook for 1–2 minutes on each side, depending on how you like it – 1 minute for medium-rare, 2 minutes for medium-well. Remove the steak and set aside on a plate or board. Remove the pan from the heat and add the butter and garlic. Let the residual heat cook the garlic for 1 minute, then pour the butter on top of the steak. Leave the steak to rest for 5 minutes while you make the salad.

Combine all the ingredients for the dressing in a large bowl and stir well.

Add the cucumber, red onion, herbs and chilli to the dressing and toss to combine.

Once the steak has rested, slice it into thin strips. Place the strips on a serving plate, covering the surface. Lightly sprinkle some flaky sea salt on top, then use a vegetable peeler to shave off large ribbons of Parmesan over the top. Finally, pile the herb salad in the middle and garnish with the burnt lemon.

CHILLI BUTTER CHICKEN WITH FENNEL SALAD

The perfect time to cook this is when summer is just around the corner or the sun is shining. A decadent soy butter is drizzled over the chicken and it's all served with a tangy, peppery herb salad. Searing the lemon in a dry pan caramelises the sugars and mellows the acid, resulting in a sweet and jammy juice when squeezed. This dish uses the 'paillard' technique of pounding the chicken with a mallet. It flattens the breast to allow for quick and even cooking.

2 skinless chicken breasts
2 tbsp olive oil
1 lime, halved
2 tbsp unsalted butter
1 red chilli, very finely chopped
3 garlic cloves, very finely chopped
1 tsp chilli powder
1 tsp MSG
1 tsp granulated sugar
salt and freshly ground black pepper
grated Parmesan, to serve

For the salad
1 fennel
juice of ½ lime
1 tbsp olive oil
1 tsp light soy sauce
pinch of salt
60g rocket
small bunch of coriander, sliced into thirds

First, prepare the salad. Using a sharp knife, cut the fennel in half, then make two diagonal cuts to remove the core at the bottom. If you have a mandoline, shave the fennel, otherwise slice it as thinly as possible using a knife.

Put the lime juice, oil, soy sauce and salt into a bowl and mix to combine. Add the fennel, then the rocket and coriander. Don't mix yet – this will stop it from wilting.

Tear off a large sheet of baking paper and place the chicken breasts on one half, then fold the other half over the top. Using a rolling pin or mallet, gently bash the chicken until flattened to around 1–2cm thick. Season with a generous pinch of salt and pepper then drizzle the oil over both sides.

Heat a frying pan over high heat for about 3 minutes. Once the pan starts to smoke, add the chicken breasts and the halved lime, cut side down. Remove the lime after 1 minute – it should look almost burnt. Cook the chicken for 3 minutes on each side, leaving it alone so that it forms a nice crust. Remove from the pan and set aside to rest.

Add the butter to the same pan over a medium-low heat, then add the chilli, garlic, chilli powder, MSG and sugar. Stir to combine, ensuring the garlic doesn't burn, for about 1 minute, or until the butter is foaming.

Put the chicken onto plates and drizzle with the butter. Grate a light covering of Parmesan on top. Toss the salad and add a generous handful on the side, then garnish with the burnt lime wedge.

GARLIC BEEF UDON SOUP

A taste of Japan right at home, this is simple, quick and easy – one of the most comforting bowls you could eat for breakfast, lunch or dinner! If possible, use frozen udon. It's just fresh udon, frozen. Big supermarkets have started stocking them, and most if not all Asian supermarkets will have them in the freezer section. You can substitute the dashi powder with any type of stock like beef, chicken or vegetable; however, if you use dashi powder, it'll taste like the authentic Japanese restaurants! If vegan, substitute the beef with fried tofu and vegetable stock and omit the egg yolk. Add chilli powder or togarashi on top if you like it spicy!

250g sirloin or rib-eye steak, very thinly sliced
1 tbsp vegetable oil
1 thumb-sized piece of fresh ginger, cut into matchsticks
2 tbsp sake
2 tbsp mirin
2 tbsp light soy sauce
2 tbsp dashi powder (or 500ml beef stock instead of the water)
500ml water
2 x 250g packets of frozen (or fresh) udon noodles
3 spring onions, sliced thinly and placed in a bowl of ice-cold water
2 medium egg yolks

For the marinade
3 garlic cloves, very finely chopped
1 tsp granulated sugar
1 tbsp light soy sauce
1 tbsp mirin
1 tsp sesame seeds
1 tsp sesame oil

Combine all the ingredients for the marinade in a bowl, then add the steak and mix together.

Heat a frying pan over a high heat for 1 minute, then add the oil and the beef, discarding any leftover marinade. Spread out the beef evenly in the pan and leave to caramelise for about 1 minute, then flip the beef over and cook for a further 1 minute. Remove from the heat and set aside.

Heat a saucepan over a high heat and add the ginger, sake, mirin, soy sauce, dashi powder (or stock) and water. Bring to the boil, then add the noodles and stir for about 3 minutes until the noodles have separated.

Divide the noodles and soup between two bowls and top with the beef. Drain the spring onions and place a mound in the middle of the beef. With your finger, make a small indent in the mounds of spring onion. Place an egg yolk in the indent in the spring onions, then serve.

SOY-GLAZED CHICKEN AND CHIVE RICE BOWL

PREP TIME 5 MINUTES
SERVES 2
COOK TIME 30 MINUTES

Sweet, sticky, SAUCY. Need I say more? If you're a fan of teriyaki, you'll love this. Glazed chicken thighs on a bed of white rice, with egg ribbons, seaweed and a heap of chives. Use the same pan the chicken is cooked in for the sauce so you can scrape up all those golden bits to maximise flavour! Comfort food at its finest.

2 medium eggs
3 tbsp vegetable oil
4 boneless chicken thighs (skinless or skin-on)
4 tbsp sake
4 tbsp mirin
2 tbsp light soy sauce
2 tbsp light brown soft sugar
1 tbsp cornflour mixed with 2 tbsp water
½ sheet of nori seaweed (optional), cut into thin strips
large bunch of chives, thinly sliced
salt and freshly ground black pepper
cooked Japanese short-grain rice (see page 23), to serve

Crack the eggs into a bowl, add a pinch of salt and whisk with a fork for about 45 seconds until the yolks and whites are fully combined.

Heat a small frying pan over a medium heat, add 1 tablespoon of the oil and swirl to cover the pan. Add half the egg mixture and swirl the pan to create a thin egg 'pancake'. Cook for 1 minute, flip over and cook for a further 30 seconds, then remove from the pan. And another tablespoon of oil and repeat the process with the remaining beaten egg, then set the two sheets of egg aside to cool. Once cool, stack the two sheets of egg on top of each other and roll into a cylinder. Slice thinly into ribbons.

Season the chicken lightly on both sides with salt and pepper. Heat the pan used for making the omelette over a high heat for about 2 minutes, then add the remaining 1 tablespoon of oil and swirl to coat the pan. Add the chicken thighs and cook for 4 minutes, then flip and cook for a further 4 minutes. Add the sake, mirin, soy sauce and sugar. Swirl the pan for 1–2 minutes until the sugar has dissolved, then flip the chicken to glaze both sides. Remove the chicken and set aside.

Turn the heat to the lowest setting and slowly pour in the cornflour and water slurry while stirring. The sauce should thicken – if it's too thick add a splash of water.

Slice the chicken into 1–2cm strips. Divide the rice between deep bowls, then top with a generous amount of nori strips and the egg ribbons. Add the sliced chicken and pour the sauce on top. Finish with a big handful of chives – the more the better!

HERBY LIME STEAK AND PICKLED ONIONS

PREP TIME 10 MINUTES
SERVES 1
COOK TIME 3 MINUTES

Flash-fried cubed rib-eye steak, perfectly pink in the middle and melt-in-your-mouth tender, drizzled with umami-rich lime mayonnaise and topped with a handful of crunchy herbs and tangy pickled onions to cut through the richness. This goes perfectly with a bowl of steaming hot rice.

250g rib-eye steak, cut into 2.5–5cm cubes
1 garlic clove, very finely chopped
1 tbsp light soy sauce
1 tbsp oyster sauce
½ tsp granulated sugar
1 tsp freshly ground black pepper
4 tbsp vegetable oil
cooked Japanese short-grain rice (see page 23), to serve

For the herb salad
small bunch of coriander, roughly chopped
small bunch of Thai basil, roughly chopped
small bunch of mint, roughly chopped
2 spring onions, roughly chopped
½ tsp salt
1 tsp olive oil

For the pickled red onions
90ml rice vinegar (or any white vinegar)
1 star anise
½ teaspoon salt
1 tsp granulated sugar
1 red onion, very thinly sliced

For the lime mayonnaise
1 tbsp Japanese mayo, such as Kewpie (or regular mayo)
zest and juice of 1 lime
1 tsp light soy sauce
1 tsp wasabi paste

Put all the ingredients for the herb salad into a bowl and toss to combine, then set aside.

To make the pickled red onions, combine the rice vinegar, star anise, salt and sugar in a bowl. Stir until the sugar has dissolved. Add the red onion, making sure it is submerged fully. Set aside.

In a third bowl, combine all the ingredients for the lime mayonnaise. Stir to combine, then set aside.

Put the steak and garlic into a bowl, followed by the soy sauce, oyster sauce, sugar, black pepper and 1 tablespoon of the oil. Mix well to coat the steak.

Heat a large, dry frying pan or wok over a high heat for 2 minutes, or until the pan is smoking. Add the remaining oil and swirl to coat the pan, then add the steak and flash-fry for 1 minute, making sure to shake the pan constantly.

Grab a shallow bowl and add the steak. Pour the lime mayonnaise on top, followed by a large handful of the herb salad in the middle. Finally, using a fork or chopsticks, fish out the pickled red onions and place around the herbs. Enjoy with a bowl of rice.

KIMCHI AND GARLIC CHICKEN QUESADILLAS WITH CHIVE BUTTER

PREP TIME 5 MINUTES
SERVES 2
COOK TIME 20 MINUTES

Nothing's better in a cheesy quesadilla than something spicy and tangy. Enter kimchi! These moreish, chicken-loaded quesadillas are toasted in a pan to crisp up the tortilla then drizzled with chive butter. Fry the chicken thighs whole, then chop them up into tiny pieces, Mexican style.

4 boneless chicken thighs
1 tsp garlic powder
½ tsp chilli powder
1 tsp medium curry powder (or mild/hot, depending on your preference)
1 tbsp light soy sauce
½ tsp MSG (optional)
½ tsp granulated sugar
2 tbsp olive oil
2 large tortilla wraps
120g mozzarella, shredded
200g kimchi, finely chopped
1 onion, finely diced
4 tbsp unsalted butter
1 tsp paprika
2 garlic cloves, finely chopped
small bunch of chives, thinly sliced
small bunch of coriander, thinly sliced
1 lime, cut into wedges
salt and freshly ground black pepper

For the avocado cream
3 tbsp sour cream
2 avocados, cubed
small bunch of coriander
pinch of salt
juice of 1 lime
1–2 tbsp water

Put the chicken thighs into a bowl with the garlic powder, chilli powder, curry powder, light soy sauce, MSG (if using), sugar, a pinch of salt, black pepper and 1 tablespoon of the olive oil. Mix well to coat thoroughly.

Next, make the avocado cream. Combine all the ingredients in a food processor and blend until smooth. Pour into a bowl and set aside.

Heat the remaining tablespoon of olive oil in a frying pan over a medium-high heat for 1–2 minutes, then gently place the chicken thighs in the pan and cook for 3–4 minutes on each side until slightly charred. Remove from the pan and leave to rest for 3–4 minutes, then chop into small pieces.

Grab a tortilla wrap and scatter half of the mozzarella on one half, spreading it all the way to the edge. Top with half the chicken, half the kimchi and half the diced onion, making sure to spread them out over the cheese. Fold the empty side of the tortilla over to close the quesadilla. Repeat with the remaining tortilla.

Melt 2 tablespoons of butter in a frying pan over a medium-high heat, then add the paprika and garlic. Cook for 2–3 minutes until fragrant, then reduce the heat to medium-low and add the chives.

Melt another tablespoon of butter in the pan and swirl to coat, then place the two folded tortillas in the pan, with the cheese on the bottom. Gently press down with your fingers. Cook for 2 minutes, then flip and add the remaining tablespoon of butter to the pan. Cook for a further 2 minutes, or until the cheese has melted and the tortilla has turned golden.

Remove the tortillas and slice them in half into triangles. Place two halves on a plate and drizzle over the garlic and chive butter. Sprinkle with the chopped coriander and garnish with lime wedges. Dip into the avocado cream or spoon onto each bite.

FORGOT TO DO A SHOP?

STORE CUPBOARD STAPLES

Late-night cravings for food always have me roaming my cupboards for something tasty, especially when the local shop is closed, and this is when the real magic happens. The best food always comes from throwing together anything and everything you happen to have to hand. In my house, this sort of meal is called a 'mish mash' – a little bit of everything from around the kitchen. From instant noodles to untouched jars of condiments, these recipes make use of everyday cupboard staples by repurposing ingredients bought for one dish, in another!

ANTI-HANGER PEANUT BUTTER CHILLI OIL NOODLES v

PREP TIME 5 MINUTES
SERVES 1
COOK TIME 8 MINUTES

Feeling a bit angry from hunger? Don't worry, these extra-saucy noodles will be ready in minutes to make you happy again! The noodles are tossed in spicy and addictive peanut butter sauce with cucumber, coriander and spring onion – get ready to slurp away those hunger pains.

1 garlic clove, very finely chopped
½ spring onion, green part only, thinly sliced
small bunch of coriander, thinly sliced
1 tsp chilli powder
½ tsp granulated sugar
½ tsp MSG (optional)
1 tsp sesame seeds
3 tbsp vegetable oil
1 tbsp smooth peanut butter
2 tsp light soy sauce
1 tsp rice vinegar
1 tsp sesame oil
1 medium egg
200g packet of fresh udon noodles
1 tbsp shop-bought fried shallots

Put the garlic, spring onion, coriander, chilli powder, sugar, MSG (if using) and sesame seeds into a bowl and stir to combine.

Heat 1 tablespoon of the oil in a frying pan over a high heat for 1–2 minutes, or until almost smoking. Pour the oil over the mixture in the bowl and stir to combine. Next, add the peanut butter, soy sauce, rice vinegar and sesame oil. Mix thoroughly and set aside.

Add the remaining oil to the frying pan and heat over a high heat for 1–2 minutes. Crack in the egg and fry for 1–2 minutes until the edges turn golden brown. Remove from the heat.

Bring a saucepan of water to the boil and cook the noodles for about 3 minutes. Add 1 tablespoon of cooking water to the peanut butter sauce, then drain the noodles and add to the bowl. Mix thoroughly to coat the noodles in sauce. Sprinkle over the fried shallots and top with the crispy fried egg.

EGG YOLK MAYO INSTANT NOODLES v

No time to make your own broth? This quick hack shows how you can use two household ingredients to turn a boring clear broth into a rich and creamy one. An egg yolk and mayonnaise are the culprits here! No extra cooking needs to be done, just cook your instant noodles as you usually do.

1 garlic clove, very finely chopped
1 tsp chilli flakes
1 tbsp vegetable oil
1 medium egg yolk
1 tbsp mayonnaise
250g packet of instant noodles (preferably Shin Ramyun, or any spicy flavour)
1 spring onion, thinly sliced
1 slice of American cheese

Put the garlic and chilli flakes into a serving bowl.

Heat the oil in a frying pan over a high heat for 1–2 minutes until smoking, then carefully pour the hot oil over the garlic and chilli flakes. Give it a stir to combine, then add the egg yolk, mayonnaise and the soup sachet that came with the noodles. Stir vigorously until well combined.

Cook the noodles according to the packet instructions, along with the flavouring sachets (I like to do 1 minute less for chewier noodles).

Once cooked, pour the noodles and their soup into the bowl with the mayo mixture and give everything a thorough stir until all the sauce at the bottom has been combined into the noodles. Top with the spring onion and slice of cheese. Enjoy!

SPICY AND SOUR SOUP NOODLES

Perfect for cold, wintery days, this quick spicy and sour comforting noodle soup will keep you warm. Throw away the salty soup sachets that come with your instant noodles and make your own instead! You can make it as mild or as spicy as you like by upping the chilli powder and use whatever noodles you have – this recipe works with all types.

2 skinless and boneless chicken thighs
1 tsp granulated sugar
1 tsp MSG
pinch of salt
1 tbsp olive oil
1 garlic clove, very finely chopped
1 spring onion, thinly sliced
small bunch of coriander, thinly sliced
1 tsp chilli powder
1 tsp sesame seeds
1 tsp ground Sichuan pepper (optional)
1 tbsp vegetable oil
1 tsp light soy sauce
1 tsp dark soy sauce
1 tsp rice vinegar
1 tsp chilli garlic sauce (I use Lee Kum Kee, or you can use sriracha)
550ml chicken stock
1 packet of instant noodles (any type)
1 pak choi, sliced into 1–2cm strips
handful of beansprouts
1 lime, cut into wedges, to serve

Put the chicken thighs into a bowl with half the sugar, half the MSG, a generous pinch of salt and the olive oil. Mix to fully coat the chicken.

Preheat a griddle pan (or frying pan) over a high heat for 2 minutes. Cook the chicken thighs for 4–5 minutes and then flip and cook for a further 2–3 minutes. Remove the chicken and set aside to rest.

Put the garlic, spring onion, coriander, chilli powder, sesame seeds, ground Sichuan pepper (if using) and the remaining sugar and MSG into a serving bowl. Heat the vegetable oil in a small saucepan over a high heat for 1–2 minutes until almost smoking, then pour the oil into the bowl with the aromatics and stir. Add the light and dark soy sauce, rice vinegar and chilli garlic sauce. Mix to combine and set aside.

Pour the chicken stock into a saucepan and bring to the boil, then add the noodles (without adding the flavouring sachets), pak choi and beansprouts and cook for 1 minute less than the time stated on the noodle packet. Once cooked, pour into the serving bowl with the sauce and give it a stir to fully combine.

Slice the chicken thighs into strips and place on top. Garnish with a small wedge of lime.

CARBONARA INSTANT NOODLES

PREP TIME 5 MINUTES
SERVES 2
COOK TIME 10 MINUTES

Look away Italians, this breaks all the rules, but it really is worth it! Think of it as a homage; the recipe uses the same authentic methods but adds a little Asian flair. Based on new trends popping up in East Asia, the combination of dairy and chilli heat really will have you coming back for more. Best of all, most of these ingredients should be in your cupboard already. Try to get hold of the thicker instant noodles – Korean brands are usually wider and chewier.

100g Parmesan, grated
1 medium egg plus 1 egg yolk
1 tbsp freshly ground black pepper
4 rashers of streaky bacon, sliced into 1cm strips
1 tbsp vegetable oil
100ml double cream
pinch of salt
2 x 150g packets of instant noodles (preferably a Korean brand)

To serve
1 sheet of nori seaweed, cut into thin strips
sesame seeds
chilli oil

Put the Parmesan, egg, egg yolk and black pepper into a bowl and use a fork to whisk to combine thoroughly, then set aside.

Put the strips of bacon into a cold frying pan. Add the oil to the pan and turn the heat to medium. Gently fry the bacon for 2–3 minutes until slightly browned, then add the cream and salt and cook for a further 1 minute. Remove from the heat and set aside.

Bring a saucepan of water to the boil and cook the noodles for 1 minute less than the time stated on the packet (without adding the flavouring sachets). Drain, reserving 5 tablespoons of the cooking water.

Heat the frying pan with the bacon over a medium heat for about 1 minute, then add the noodles and reserved cooking water and stir to combine. Remove from the heat and add the Parmesan and egg mixture. Stir vigorously until the sauce starts to thicken.

Transfer the noodles to a plate and sprinkle over the nori strips, sesame seeds and your favourite chilli oil.

CHILLI AND SESAME DUMPLING SALAD v

PREP TIME 10 MINUTES
SERVES 2
COOK TIME 7 MINUTES

Frozen dumplings to the rescue! Whoever invented them deserves a medal because after a long day, they really are life savers. Gyoza-type pan-seared dumplings work the best here. Tossed in a chilli, vinegar and sesame dressing with lots of herbs and vegetables, the only cooking done is the dumplings!

1 cucumber, roughly chopped
1 tsp salt
1 tbsp vegetable oil
200g frozen dumplings of your choice
50ml water
4 romaine lettuce leaves, shredded
75g cherry tomatoes, halved
1 spring onion, thinly sliced
small bunch of coriander, thinly sliced
small bunch of chives, thinly sliced
small bunch of mint, thinly sliced

For the dressing
1 tbsp chilli oil
3 tbsp tahini
1 tbsp light soy sauce
2 tbsp rice vinegar
1 tsp sesame oil
1 tsp granulated sugar
1 tbsp water

To serve
1 tbsp roasted and salted peanuts, chopped
1 tbsp sesame seeds
1 tsp chilli oil

Combine the cucumber and salt in a bowl, mix to coat well and set aside for 5 minutes. The salt will draw the excess moisture from the cucumber. Drain the excess liquid, then place the cucumber back into the bowl.

Combine the ingredients for the dressing in a large bowl and set aside.

Heat the vegetable oil in a frying pan over a medium heat, then fry the dumplings for 3–4 minutes, or until golden on the bottom. Add the water and cover, then cook for a further 3 minutes, or until the water has completely evaporated. Remove the lid and cook for a further 1 minute.

Add all the remaining ingredients to the bowl with the dressing, then add the dumplings and toss well. Transfer to plates, then sprinkle with the peanuts and sesame seeds. Drizzle with the chilli oil and enjoy.

TWENTY-CLOVE GARLIC NOODLES

PREP TIME 8 MINUTES
SERVES 2
COOK TIME 20 MINUTES

When East meets West, we get this love affair between garlic and pasta. Found in many East Asian restaurants, these extremely garlicky noodles are usually paired with lobster or crab but, to me, they're perfect with some crispy fried eggs. Works with chicken or prawns, as a side or a main, it's up to you to get creative. The more Parmesan, the better, obviously!

2½ tbsp unsalted butter
20 garlic cloves, very finely chopped
1 banana shallot, finely diced
small bunch of chives, thinly sliced
1 tbsp oyster sauce
1 tsp light soy sauce
1 tsp fish sauce
½ tsp granulated sugar
1 tsp freshly ground black pepper
200g spaghetti or 240g fresh egg noodles
pinch of salt
2–3 tbsp vegetable oil
2 medium eggs
100g Parmesan, grated
1 tsp chilli powder

Melt the butter in a frying pan over a medium-high heat, then fry the garlic and shallot for 2–3 minutes until fragrant but not browned. Add the chives, oyster sauce, soy sauce, fish sauce, sugar and black pepper. Stir to combine. Remove 2 teaspoons of the garlic butter and set aside for garnishing.

Bring a large saucepan of water to the boil and season with the salt. Cook the spaghetti or noodles for 2 minutes less than the time stated on the packet. Meanwhile, cook the fried eggs.

Heat the oil in a small frying pan over a high heat for 1–2 minutes, then fry the eggs for 1 minute until the edges are crispy but the yolk is still runny. Remove from the heat.

Once cooked, drain the spaghetti or noodles, reserving the cooking water, then immediately add them to the pan with the garlic butter. Place the pan over a medium heat, add the Parmesan and stir vigorously. Add a ladle of cooking water and keep stirring to emulsify the cheese into the sauce. If it looks too dry, add another ladle of water.

Transfer the spaghetti or noodles to a serving plate and top with the eggs to one side. Spoon the reserved garlic butter over the eggs. Finally, sprinkle over the chilli powder.

BRAISED CABBAGE AND GARLIC NOODLES

PREP TIME 10 MINUTES
SERVES 2
COOK TIME 17 MINUTES

Not a single thing reminds me of home more than this dish. Tons of garlic, toasted in oil until golden brown and jammy, then mixed with glass noodles and cabbage and braised in umami-rich soy sauce until soft. It's what got my greens in my belly, so no wonder my mum made it so often! As a child, it was an obsession of mine and still is.

8 garlic cloves, smashed
2 tbsp vegetable oil
2 thin slices of fresh ginger, cut into matchsticks
1 bird's eye chilli, sliced in half (optional)
2 x 50g nests of glass noodles
400ml vegetable or chicken stock
4 Chinese leaf leaves, thinly sliced
5 shiitake mushrooms, stems removed and sliced
100g medium-firm tofu, diced
handful of beansprouts
½ carrot, sliced into matchsticks
3 spring onions, green and white parts separated and thinly sliced
small bunch of coriander, thinly sliced

For the seasoning
1 tbsp light soy sauce
1 tbsp dark soy sauce
1 tsp fish sauce
1 tbsp oyster sauce
1 tsp sesame oil
1 tbsp sesame seeds
1 tsp light brown soft sugar
½ tsp ground white pepper
pinch of MSG (optional)

To serve
1 tbsp shop-bought fried shallots
1 lime, cut into wedges

First, combine all the ingredients for the seasoning in a small bowl and mix well. Set aside.

Put the garlic and oil into a cold medium-small saucepan and turn the heat to medium. Fry for 3–5 minutes until soft and golden brown. Add the ginger and chilli and fry for a further 1 minute, then add all the remaining ingredients except the green parts of the spring onions and the coriander. Pour in the seasoning and stir. Cover and bring to the boil, then reduce the heat to medium-low and cook for 6–8 minutes, stirring once or twice, until the liquid has reduced by half. Add the green parts of the spring onions and the coriander, stir to combine, cover again and cook for a further 2 minutes.

Divide between shallow bowls, then sprinkle with the fried shallots and garnish with a wedge of lime.

KIMCHI EGG RIBBON UDON SOUP v

PREP TIME 5 MINUTES
SERVES 2
COOK TIME 15 MINUTES

Think tomato soup but with a spicy, tangy punch – and chewy udon noodles of course! This soup noodle dish is really so simple that it's as easy as making instant noodles. Thinly sliced omelette is the choice of protein. This is a traditional East Asian way of cooking egg as a garnish that creates long ribbons, almost like noodles. A mountain of spring onion to finish it off, because why not? Lastly, a raw egg yolk on top – when mixed in it gives the soup a creamy, rich texture.

2 medium eggs, plus 2 egg yolks
pinch of salt
3 tbsp vegetable oil
2 spring onions
½ white onion, thinly sliced
2 leaves of Chinese leaf, thinly sliced
4 tbsp kimchi
500ml vegetable stock
1 tbsp light soy sauce
1 tsp granulated sugar
250g packet of frozen (or fresh) udon noodles

Crack 2 of the eggs into a bowl, add a pinch of salt and whisk with a fork for about 45 seconds until the yolks and whites are fully combined.

Heat a small frying pan over a medium heat, add 1 tablespoon of the oil and swirl to cover the pan. Add half the egg mixture and swirl the pan to create a thin egg 'pancake'. Cook for 1 minute, then flip over and cook for a further 30 seconds, then remove from the pan. And another tablespoon of oil and repeat the process with the remaining beaten egg, then set the two sheets of egg aside to cool. Once cool, stack one sheet of egg on top of the other and roll into a cylinder. Slice thinly into ribbons.

Slice the spring onions as thinly as possible and then place them in a bowl of cold water (add ice if you have it). Set aside.

Heat a saucepan over a medium heat for about 1 minute, then add the remaining tablespoon of oil and the onion, Chinese leaf and kimchi and sauté for 2 minutes. Add the stock, soy sauce and sugar and whack the heat up to high until the soup comes to the boil. Once boiling, add the egg ribbons and noodles and gently shake the noodles to separate them. Cook for 3 minutes, then pour into bowls.

Drain the spring onion and add half on top of each bowl. With your finger, make a small indent in the mounds of spring onion. Place an egg yolk in the indent in the spring onions, then serve.

BURNT SPRING ONION UDON v

PREP TIME 5 MINUTES
SERVES 2
COOK TIME 15 MINUTES

A super-simple, soy-glazed noodle dish. The sauce is cooked using the residual heat of the pan, which concentrates the flavour, giving it a sweet and salty profile. Add a crispy fried egg on top if you like, and feel free to substitute the udon for any other type of noodle!

150g beansprouts
large bunch of chives, thinly sliced
1 tsp light soy sauce
1 tbsp sesame oil
1 tsp chilli flakes
2 tbsp sesame seeds
2 x 250g packets of frozen (or fresh) udon noodles
2 tbsp vegetable oil
2 spring onions, cut into thirds
1 banana shallot, halved
1 thick slice of ginger

For the sauce
1 tbsp light soy sauce
3 tbsp dark soy sauce
1 tbsp vegetarian oyster sauce (or oyster sauce)
1 tbsp granulated sugar
1 tsp MSG
2 tbsp vegetable oil

Bring a saucepan of water to the boil and cook the beansprouts for 3 minutes, then remove with a slotted spoon and place in a bowl. Add the chives, soy sauce, sesame oil, chilli flakes and sesame seeds. Mix well, then set aside.

Put the noodles into the same pan of boiling water and cook for about 3 minutes until the noodles have separated, then drain and set aside.

In a bowl, combine all the ingredients for the sauce and mix well until the sugar has dissolved.

Heat a frying pan over a medium for about 1 minute, then add the oil. Add the spring onions, shallot and ginger and cook for 5 minutes until the spring onions turn a dark colour. Transfer the spring onions to a plate and discard the ginger and shallot.

Increase the heat to high and allow the pan to heat up for about 30 seconds until smoking, then turn the heat off. Stir the sauce and pour it into the pan. This technique will concentrate and caramelise the sauce.
Add the noodles to the pan and mix well.

Transfer the noodles to a plate and add a handful of the beansprouts on top, followed by some of the reserved crispy spring onions. Enjoy!

CHEESE AND SPAM INSTANT NOODLE HOTPOT

PREP TIME 20 MINUTES · SERVES 2 · COOK TIME 15 MINUTES

Nothing beats sitting around a communal hotpot of spicy noodles with friends and family, dipping sauce and beer in hand – it's the true backbone of South and Southeast Asian food culture! Beware though, it's a free for all. If you don't eat quickly, you don't eat! This is a kitchen-raid style dish, so whatever you have lying around, chuck it in!

1 x 200g tin of Spam, sliced lengthways into 1cm pieces
2 frankfurters, sliced diagonally
2 Chinese leaf leaves, sliced into 3–4cm chunks
100g enoki mushrooms (optional)
100g shiitake mushrooms, stems removed and thinly sliced
1 onion, sliced into rounds
200g firm tofu, cubed
100g kimchi, sliced
400ml chicken stock
2 x 120g packets of instant noodles
4 slices of American cheese
handful of beansprouts
2 medium eggs
4 spring onions, thinly sliced

For the hotpot sauce
2 tbsp mirin
1 tbsp light soy sauce
½ tbsp granulated sugar
1 tbsp gochugaru (Korean red pepper flakes; or 1 tsp cayenne pepper and 1 tsp paprika)
1 tbsp gochujang paste
1 garlic clove, finely chopped
½ tsp freshly ground black pepper

For the dipping sauce
2 tbsp sesame oil
2 tbsp light soy sauce
1 tbsp oyster sauce
1 tbsp rice vinegar
1 tsp granulated sugar
1 tbsp sesame seeds
small bunch of coriander, thinly sliced
2 spring onions, thinly sliced
1 banana shallot, finely diced
2 garlic cloves, finely chopped
1 red chilli, finely chopped

First, prepare the hotpot sauce. Mix together all the ingredients in a bowl until thoroughly combined and set aside.

Next, make the dipping sauce. Combine all the wet ingredients in a bowl with the sugar and sesame seeds and stir until the sugar has dissolved, then add the coriander, spring onions, shallot, garlic and chilli. Mix thoroughly to combine and then set aside.

Now prepare the hotpot. Arrange the Spam, frankfurters, Chinese leaf, mushrooms, onion, tofu and kimchi in a large, heavy-based shallow pan, placing each ingredient against the edge of the pan in its own area and making sure there is a space in the middle. Pour the hotpot sauce into the middle followed by the chicken stock. Turn the heat to high and cover, then bring to the boil and cook for 5–7 minutes.

Remove the lid and place the noodles, cheese and beansprouts in the middle. Crack the eggs into a space where there is some liquid. Cook, uncovered, for 3 minutes, or until the noodles are ready. Heap the sliced spring onions into the middle of the pan and serve.

Place the bowl of dipping sauce on the table, so that you can spoon some into your own bowl. Grab whatever ingredients you fancy, place into your dipping sauce and enjoy.

SPICY MISO GRILLED CABBAGE

PREP TIME 5 MINUTES
SERVES 2
COOK TIME 20 MINUTES

A dish made for hot summer days, this grilled cabbage is doused in a spicy miso butter and nestled on a bed of coriander yoghurt and crispy chorizo. The lime juice helps to balance out the richness of the miso paste. This is a great starter to share with friends or enjoy by yourself with a bowl of steamed rice.

1½ tbsp unsalted butter
2 tbsp mirin
1 tbsp miso paste
1 tsp chilli oil
juice of 1 lime
3 tbsp olive oil
75g chorizo, diced
pinch of salt
1 tsp freshly ground black pepper
1 sweetheart (pointed/hispi) cabbage, quartered
small bunch of chives, thinly sliced

For the coriander yoghurt
450g Greek yoghurt
small bunch of coriander, thinly sliced
1 spring onion, finely chopped
zest of 1 lime
pinch of salt

First, make the coriander yoghurt. Combine all the ingredients in a bowl and mix well. Set aside.

Melt the butter in a frying pan over a medium-high heat, then add the mirin, miso paste, chilli oil and lime juice. Whisk until combined and cook for 1 minute, then remove from the heat and set aside.

Heat 1 tablespoon of the oil in a separate frying pan over a medium-high heat and fry the chorizo for 3–4 minutes until crispy. Set aside.

Preheat a griddle pan over a high heat. While it is heating, prepare the cabbage by rubbing the remaining oil, salt and pepper over each piece, making sure to get in all the cracks.

Place the cabbage quarters on the griddle pan and cook for about 3 minutes on each side until well charred. Remove the cabbage and brush on the miso paste all over.

Spread out the coriander yoghurt on a serving plate, then spoon over the chorizo pieces and their oil. Place the cabbage on top and sprinkle over the chives.

GOCHUJANG PRAWN PASTA BAKE

This is a spicy twist on a classic pasta bake, with a bit of Korean flair! All you need to do is half-cook the pasta and prawns, and the oven will do the rest. It also works well with chicken, or for a vegetarian version, just omit the prawns altogether.

175g fusilli
75g broccoli, finely chopped
2 tbsp olive oil
4 garlic cloves, thinly sliced
2 tbsp gochujang paste
100ml double cream
165g raw peeled king prawns
4 tbsp mascarpone
1 tsp granulated sugar
150g ball of mozzarella, torn
5 tbsp grated Parmesan
large bunch of chives, finely chopped
salt

Preheat the oven to 240°C/220°C fan/gas mark 9.

Bring a saucepan of water to the boil and add a generous pinch of salt, then add the pasta and broccoli and cook for half the time stated on the pasta packet. Drain and set aside.

Heat a frying pan over a medium heat, then add the oil and garlic. Fry for 30 seconds until soft and slightly coloured, then add the gochujang and fry for a further 1 minute until the oil turns a reddish hue. Add the cream and mix to combine, then add the prawns, followed by the pasta and mascarpone. Season with a pinch of salt and the sugar and mix thoroughly.

Pour the mixture into a small, deep baking dish, about 10 x 25cm. Cover the top of the pasta with the torn mozzarella, then with the Parmesan, ensuring every bit is covered.

Put the dish into the oven and bake for 20 minutes, or until golden brown on top. Remove from the oven and sprinkle with the chives before serving.

FIRECRACKER RICE

A 'fridge raid'-style red curry fried rice using shop-bought curry paste – a restaurant secret, shhh! The beautiful thing about this is that all the hard work is done for you in the curry paste, so it's a failsafe recipe. Plus, it comes together in no time – once the ingredients are prepped and the pan is on, it's all hands on deck. Go easy on the seasonings as the curry paste will already have bags of flavour. Chuck in any vegetables or protein you have lying about in your fridge – there are no rules, anything goes!

1 tbsp blanched peanuts
3 tbsp vegetable oil
1 banana shallot, finely chopped
3 cloves garlic, very finely chopped
2 tbsp Thai red curry paste
2 skinless and boneless chicken thighs, cut into bite-sized pieces
370g cooked jasmine rice (see page 23)
2 medium eggs
1 tsp granulated sugar
1 tsp light soy sauce
1 tsp fish sauce
handful of coriander
1 spring onion, thinly sliced
1 lime, cut into wedges

Toast the peanuts in a small frying pan over a medium heat for 1 minute. If you have a pestle and mortar, transfer the peanuts to the mortar and crush them. If not, chop them into chunks with a knife.

Heat a large frying pan or wok over a high heat and add 2 tablespoons of the oil. Heat for about 1 minute, then add the shallot and garlic and stir-fry for 30 seconds. Add the red curry paste and fry for a further minute until the oil turns a reddish hue. Add the chicken, mix to coat and then cook for 2–3 minutes until the chicken starts to brown. Add the rice and stir-fry for 3 minutes, mixing thoroughly and making sure to break up any lumps.

Push the rice to one side, add the remaining tablespoon of oil and crack in the eggs. Gently scramble and fold the eggs, then once the egg is half-cooked, mix everything together. Add the sugar and then pour the soy sauce and fish sauce along the sides of the pan. Toss in the coriander and spring onion and stir vigorously for a further minute.

Transfer the rice to a bowl and top with a wedge of lime and the peanuts.

KEEPING IT LIGHT?

FRESH & HEALTHY(ISH)

I try to keep it healthy but sometimes there are days when I eat with my eyes and not my stomach. Maybe it was too many burgers or a little (big) trip to the pub . . . Either way, life is all about balance and that means it's time for some light, refreshing food so I can do it all again! Superfoods this, superfoods that . . . It's easy to get tunnel vision about what's considered healthy. These recipes demonstrate how accessible real, healthy foods are at home – it doesn't have to be all avocado, quinoa and salads!

GINGER-SOY CEVICHE

This is my version of a ceviche, with a Japanese-inspired sashimi-style twist. Although traditional ceviches are made with raw seafood, this one uses cooked prawns, which saves you worrying about handling and eating the raw stuff. The secret ingredient is homemade chilli oil. Grated ginger and garlic are steeped in lime juice and soy to give it an extra depth and umami. Eat it however you'd like, but I'd suggest a big bowl of tortilla chips!

1 thumb-sized piece of fresh ginger, grated
1 garlic clove, grated
juice of 3 limes plus zest of 1
2 tbsp light soy sauce
1 tbsp yuzu juice (optional)
pinch of salt
few cracks of black pepper
300g cooked peeled king prawns, quartered
½ cucumber, diced
1 pepper (any colour), diced
200g cherry tomatoes, diced
½ red onion, diced
1 jalapeño, diced
large bunch of coriander, thinly sliced
1 bag of salted tortilla chips, to serve

For the chilli oil
1 tbsp chilli flakes
1 tsp paprika
½ tsp cumin seeds
2 tbsp vegetable oil

Put the ginger, garlic, lime zest and juice, soy sauce, yuzu juice (if using), salt and black pepper into a bowl and stir to combine. Add the prawns and give it a mix again.

Next, make the chilli oil. Combine the chilli flakes, paprika and cumin seeds in a small bowl. Heat the oil in a small saucepan over a high heat until slightly smoking, then carefully pour the hot oil over the spices. Stir well to combine.

Add the cucumber, pepper, tomatoes, onion, jalapeño and coriander to the bowl with the prawns. Add the chilli oil and mix thoroughly until everything is combined.

Transfer to a shallow bowl and serve with your favourite tortilla chips.

WHITE BEAN AND LEEK MISO SOUP v

PREP TIME 5 MINUTES
SERVES 2
COOK TIME 20 MINUTES

A one-pan, cupboard-staple nourishing vegan soup that's packed with protein and made in minutes – quicker than boiling pasta. It's all in the prep! A drizzle of chilli oil and squeeze of lemon is all that's needed to finish off this dish, which is perfect for any day of the year. Just use your favourite shop-bought chilli oil! You can also use chicken or beef stock if you prefer, and substitute the dill with any other leafy herbs like parsley or coriander.

2 tbsp olive oil
½ onion, finely chopped
½ leek, sliced into 1cm rings
1 potato, peeled and diced into thumb-sized cubes
½ x 400g tin of cannellini beans, drained
600ml vegetable stock
1 tbsp miso paste
few sprigs of dill, thinly sliced
1 tsp chilli oil
1 lemon, cut into wedges

Heat the oil in a saucepan over medium heat, then add the onion, leek and potato and stir for 2–3 minutes until softened.

Add the beans and stir for a further minute, then add the stock and miso paste and cover. Increase the heat to high and bring to the boil, then reduce the heat to medium-low and cook for 15 minutes, or until the potato is fork-tender. Remove from the heat and stir in the dill.

Serve in a deep bowl, drizzled with your favourite chilli oil and garnished with a wedge of lemon.

SPICY SESAME GREEN SALAD v

I'm absolutely obsessed with this salad. Plenty of greens and herbs are coated in the most delicious spicy sesame dressing made with tahini and balsamic vinegar – it's sweet, salty, spicy and sour. Combining tahini with sesame oil mimics traditional Chinese sesame sauce.

150g Tenderstem broccoli
100g frozen peas
½ Chinese leaf, cut into 2–3cm chunks
1 spring onion, thinly sliced
small bunch of coriander, thinly sliced

For the dressing
1 tsp chilli powder
1 tbsp sesame seeds
½ tsp salt
1 tbsp vegetable oil
1 tbsp tahini
1 tbsp sesame oil
1 tbsp light soy sauce
3 tbsp clear honey
3 tbsp balsamic vinegar
1 tsp light brown soft sugar

Put the chilli powder, sesame seeds and salt into a large bowl.

Heat the oil in a small saucepan over a high heat for 1–2 minutes until hot but not smoking, then pour the oil into the bowl and stir to combine. Add the tahini, sesame oil, soy sauce, honey, balsamic vinegar and sugar. Stir well until combined.

Bring a saucepan of water to the boil, then cook the Tenderstem broccoli and peas for 1–2 minutes. Drain and run under cold water for 1 minute. Chop the broccoli into thirds, diagonally.

Add the broccoli, peas, Chinese leaf, spring onion and coriander to the sesame dressing and toss until fully coated.

SHREDDED CHICKEN NOODLE SALAD

Inspired by my travels in Vietnam and my love of spicy food, this summery dish is served at room temperature and hits every taste bud. Spicy, sour, salty, sweet and fragrant, I can't lie, it's addictive! Garlic oil is poured over dark soy-soaked noodles, then crispy leeks are sprinkled on top, and loads of fresh herbs bring the dish together. The perfect recipe for those unbearable heatwaves!

150g rice noodles
500ml boiling water
5 tbsp dark soy sauce
6 tbsp vegetable oil
4 garlic cloves, thinly sliced
2 skinless chicken breasts
½ leek, cut into matchsticks
pinch of salt
small bunch of coriander, roughly chopped
small bunch of mint, roughly chopped
small bunch of Thai basil, roughly chopped
½ cucumber, thinly sliced
1 celery stick, thinly sliced diagonally
½ red onion, thinly sliced
2 tbsp roasted unsalted peanuts, chopped
2 tbsp shop-bought fried shallots

For the dressing
2 bird's eye chillies
2 garlic cloves
6 tbsp fish sauce
4 tbsp rice vinegar
juice of 1 lime
6 tbsp granulated sugar

Put the rice noodles into a bowl and cover with the boiling water. Add the dark soy sauce and stir, then set aside to soak for 10 minutes.

Meanwhile, heat half the oil in a small frying pan over a medium heat for 1–2 minutes. Add the garlic and stir for 1 minute, or until lightly golden but not burnt.

Drain the noodles and then transfer them back into the bowl. Pour over the garlic and oil and toss to combine.

Bring a saucepan of water to the boil and add the chicken breasts, then lower the heat, cover and cook for 10 minutes. Remove the chicken and set aside to cool, reserving 90ml of the cooking water.

Next, make the dressing. Pound the chillies with the garlic cloves in a mortar and pestle, or chop them finely with a knife. In a bowl, combine the fish sauce, rice vinegar, lime juice, sugar, reserved cooking water and pounded chilli and garlic. Stir thoroughly until the sugar has dissolved, then set aside.

Heat the remaining oil in a frying pan over a medium heat for around 2 minutes, then add the leek and fry for 5 minutes, stirring occasionally, until golden brown. Remove from the pan and sprinkle with the salt.

Put the herbs, cucumber, celery and red onion into a large bowl. Using your fingers, shred the chicken into strips and add to the bowl. Toss the salad until thoroughly combined.

Divide the garlic noodles between plates. Grab a generous handful of the chicken salad and place on top. Sprinkle with the peanuts, fried shallots and finally the fried leeks. Give the dressing a stir and generously pour over the top, then mix well before eating.

SAKE GRILLED WINGS WITH SALT AND LIME

PREP TIME 5 MINUTES
SERVES 2
COOK TIME 20 MINUTES

When I was travelling in Japan, I came across what looked like average-looking grilled chicken wings – but oh how wrong I was. They epitomised the Japanese foundations of flavour, where less is more. These wings are influenced by that experience, and while they may sound simple, they accentuate each ingredient to the max. Marinated in sake, basted in mirin, rested and then served with a squeeze of lime and some flaky sea salt . . . trust me! If you have a charcoal barbecue, use it, but the recipe below uses the oven grill for ease.

1kg chicken wings
5 tbsp sake
2 tbsp granulated sugar
2 tbsp MSG (optional)
2 tbsp mirin
large bunch of chives, thinly sliced
3 limes, cut into wedges
2 tbsp sea salt flakes

Put the chicken wings into a large bowl and pour over the sake. Mix well to coat the wings, then set aside. If you have time, cover and marinate in the fridge for 1 hour.

Preheat your grill to maximum heat.

Meanwhile, put the sugar and MSG into a small bowl and mix well to combine. Put the mirin into a bowl.

Spread the wings out on a wire rack over a baking tray (if you don't have a wire rack, just put them directly onto the baking tray) and adjust the oven shelf so that the wings will sit directly below the grill. Place the wings under the grill and cook for 10 minutes, then flip the wings and cook for a further 7 minutes.

Remove the wings from the oven and brush them with the mirin, then sprinkle generously with the sugar and MSG mixture. Place them back under the grill for 2 more minutes.

Remove the wings and sprinkle them with the chives, then leave to rest for 5 minutes.

Transfer the wings to a plate, add a generous heap of sea salt on the side and the lime wedges around the edge. When eating, squeeze some lime juice onto a wing and generously dip the corner into the salt.

TANGY INSTANT NOODLE SALAD

PREP TIME 10 MINUTES
SERVES 1
COOK TIME 15 MINUTES

When I was in Bangkok, I found these small carts selling bowls of warm instant noodle salad tossed in a spicy and tangy lime sauce. They had an assortment of toppings and additions to choose from, ranging from different cuts of meat and seafood to vegetables and herbs! I've tried to recreate my favourite combinations here.

1 tbsp jasmine rice
1 tbsp vegetable oil
100g minced chicken
1 garlic clove, very finely chopped
1 packet of instant noodles (any type)
10g carrot, cut into matchsticks
10g cucumber, thinly sliced
3 cherry tomatoes, halved
¼ celery stick, thinly sliced
¼ red onion, thinly sliced
1 spring onion, thinly sliced
small bunch of coriander, roughly chopped
small bunch of mint, leaves picked
1 tbsp shop-bought fried shallots
1 tbsp roasted peanuts, crushed

For the dressing
1 lemongrass stalk, very finely chopped (bottom half only)
1 red chilli, very finely chopped
1 garlic clove, very finely chopped
juice of 2 limes
1 tsp granulated sugar
1 tsp light soy sauce
3 tsp fish sauce

First, make the dressing by combining all the ingredients in a large bowl. Stir until the sugar has combined, then set aside.

Put the rice into a dry frying pan over a medium heat and toast for 3–4 minutes, shaking the pan regularly. Once golden brown, transfer to a pestle and mortar and pound until ground but not too fine. Alternatively, use a spice grinder or small food processor.

Heat a frying pan over a high heat for 1–2 minutes, then add the oil, followed by the chicken and garlic. Fry for 5 minutes until the chicken is golden brown and cooked through. Add the chicken, oil and all, to the bowl with the dressing.

Bring a saucepan of water to the boil and cook the noodles (without adding the flavouring sachets) for 1 minute less than the time stated on the packet, then drain and add to the bowl, followed by the rice powder, carrot, cucumber, tomatoes, celery, red onion, spring onion, coriander and mint leaves. Toss the noodles until thoroughly combined.

Transfer to a serving plate and sprinkle with fried shallots and roasted peanuts to serve.

BAKED HONEY AND SESAME CHICKEN WITH CORIANDER AND MINT SLAW

Sticky honey-basted baked chicken thighs are one of my go-to recipes when I just don't have the capacity to stand up and cook. Whack it in the oven and quickly make the slaw, then sit down and relax while the oven does the hard work! The basting mixture is just a simple combination of honey and water, which provides that sticky, caramelised goodness you find on Chinese roast meats. The technique of salting the vegetables draws out the water to preserve their crunch.

6 skin-on boneless chicken thighs
2 tbsp clear honey
1 tbsp Chinese five-spice powder
1 tbsp light soy sauce
1 tbsp dark soy sauce
1 tbsp oyster sauce
1 tsp granulated sugar
1 tsp MSG (optional)
pinch of salt
1 tsp sesame oil
1 tsp vegetable oil
2 tbsp water
1 tbsp sesame seeds
chilli oil, to serve (optional)

For the coriander and mint slaw
½ cucumber, cut into matchsticks
½ carrot, cut into matchsticks
¼ white cabbage, thinly sliced
½ red onion, thinly sliced
small bunch of coriander, roughly chopped
small bunch of mint, roughly chopped
2 tsp mayonnaise
1 tsp rice vinegar
1 tsp light soy sauce
juice of 1 lime
salt

Preheat the oven to 200°C/180°C fan/gas mark 6.

Place the chicken on a board skin side down and use a fork to poke holes in the flesh. Transfer the chicken to a bowl and add half the honey, the five-spice powder, light and dark soy sauce, oyster sauce, sugar, MSG, salt, sesame oil and vegetable oil. Mix well to coat the chicken.

Line a baking tray with foil and place the chicken on top, skin side up. Cook in the oven for 20 minutes.

Meanwhile, put the cucumber, carrot and cabbage into a bowl with a generous pinch of salt and mix to combine. Set aside for 5 minutes. After 5 minutes, squeeze the vegetables to remove the excess water. Add the red onion, coriander and mint to the bowl.

In a separate bowl, combine the mayonnaise, rice vinegar, soy sauce, lime juice and a pinch of salt. Mix well to combine. Pour the dressing into the bowl and toss well until evenly coated.

Put the remaining tablespoon of honey into a small bowl with the water and stir until combined. Once the chicken has cooked for 20 minutes, remove it from the oven and brush or spoon some of the honey mixture over it. Return the chicken to the oven for a further 15 minutes, repeating the basting process every 5 minutes.

Once cooked, remove the chicken from the oven and liberally sprinkle with the sesame seeds. Allow to rest for 3–5 minutes before serving with the slaw. Drizzle with your favourite chilli oil if you like.

GARLIC BUTTER SALMON BITES

PREP TIME 10 MINUTES
SERVES 2
COOK TIME 20 MINUTES

You know those lazy days on the sofa when you just want a plate of food that you can eat with a spoon and nothing else? Well, this is for them. Welcome to the sofa-dinner recipe of dreams! These bite-sized blackened salmon chunks are quickly seared in a scorching hot pan and then served on a bed of rice with a crispy fried egg, chilli cucumber pickle and creamy gochujang sauce.

2 x 150g salmon fillets, cut into 5cm cubes
1 tbsp garlic powder
1 tsp chilli flakes
1 tbsp paprika
½ tsp freshly ground black pepper
pinch of salt
2 tbsp unsalted butter
3 garlic cloves, very finely chopped
small bunch of chives, thinly sliced
1 lemon, cut into wedges
cooked jasmine rice (see page 23), to serve

For the chilli cucumber pickle
1 cucumber, thinly sliced
1 tsp salt
1 garlic clove, very finely chopped
1 tsp gochugaru (Korean red pepper flakes; or chilli flakes)
1 tbsp light soy sauce
2 tbsp rice vinegar
1 tsp sesame oil
1 tsp chilli oil
1 tsp granulated sugar
1 tbsp sesame seeds
small bunch of coriander, chopped

For the sauce
1 tbsp gochujang paste
1 tsp granulated sugar
1 tbsp light soy sauce
1 tsp freshly ground black pepper
200ml single cream
pinch of salt

First, make the chilli cucumber pickle. Combine the cucumber and salt in a bowl, mix to coat well and set aside for 5 minutes. The salt will draw the excess moisture from the cucumber. Squeeze the cucumber over the sink to drain the excess liquid, pour out the liquid from the bowl and then place the cucumber back into the bowl. Add all the remaining ingredients, mix thoroughly until the sugar has dissolved, then set aside.

In a bowl, season the salmon cubes with the garlic powder, chilli flakes, paprika, pepper and salt. Toss to coat well.

Melt the butter in a frying pan over a high heat, then fry the garlic for 1–2 minutes, before adding the salmon cubes and cooking for 3–5 minutes, flipping regularly, until well browned on all sides. Transfer to a plate and pour over the butter from the pan.

Place the pan back over a medium heat, add the ingredients for the sauce and cook for 3–5 minutes, or until the cream is simmering. Remove from the heat.

Divide the rice between plates, then top with the salmon bites. Place the cucumber on the side, then drizzle the salmon and rice with the sauce. Finally, sprinkle with the chives and garnish with a wedge of lemon.

CORIANDER CHUTNEY BEEF TATAKI

PREP TIME 10 MINUTES
COOK TIME 8 MINUTES
SERVES 2

In East Asia, they have a love for rare meats – and so do I! Paired with rice or as a starter, this one will definitely impress. The beef is seared for seconds to cook it to rare perfection and then sliced as thinly as possible, similar to carpaccio. Pouring hot oil over the ginger- and garlic-brushed beef renders the delicately marbled beef fat for extra texture and flavour. The star of the show is the coriander chutney, though, which is sweet, sour and spicy. Wrap each slice with nutty cress almost like a beef sushi roll. Nothing beats it on a summer's day with an ice-cold beer!

400g fillet steak
2 tbsp light soy sauce
1 thumb-sized piece of fresh ginger
1 garlic clove
1 tbsp water
2 tbsp vegetable oil
2 tbsp extra virgin olive oil
1 tbsp sesame oil
handful of cress
salt and freshly ground black pepper
lime wedges, to serve

For the coriander chutney
large bunch of coriander
large bunch of mint
1 banana shallot, roughly chopped
1 red chilli, roughly chopped
1 tbsp sesame oil
1 tbsp light brown soft sugar
1 tbsp rice vinegar
zest of 1 lime plus juice of ½
pinch of salt

Put the steak on a plate and rub it with the light soy sauce, a pinch of salt and some black pepper. Set aside while you make the chutney.

Put all the ingredients for the coriander chutney into a food processor and blend until smooth, then set aside in a bowl.

Clean out the food processor, then add the ginger, garlic and water. Blend and set aside.

Heat the vegetable oil in a frying pan over a high heat for about 3 minutes, or until smoking. Add the steak and fry 1 minute on each side, making sure to sear every part. Stand the steak up to sear the ends for 30 seconds on each side. Remove and set aside to rest for 2 minutes.

Once rested, slice the steak as thinly as possible. Divide the steak between plates and use the back of a spoon to brush it with the garlic and ginger paste. Heat the olive oil and sesame oil in a frying pan over a medium heat for about 3 minutes, or until smoking. Carefully pour the oil over the steak. Place a handful of cress and a couple of wedges of lime on top of the beef. Serve with the chutney.

SEARED SEA BASS AND ONION SALAD

This light and healthy dish features crispy sea bass and a ceviche-inspired onion salad full of Peruvian and Japanese flavours. A ginger, coriander and citrus dressing is drizzled over tomatoes, cucumber and onion – the salad really is the star of the show!

4 x skin-on sea bass fillets
1 tbsp olive oil
1 tbsp unsalted butter
1 tsp paprika
1 garlic clove, very finely chopped
1 tbsp light soy sauce
1 tbsp cooking sake (optional)
salt and freshly ground black pepper

For the salad
½ cucumber, thinly sliced
1 tsp salt
½ red onion, thinly sliced
small bunch of coriander, leaves picked and stalks thinly sliced
handful of cherry tomatoes, halved
zest and juice of 1 lime
zest and juice of 1 lemon
2cm piece of fresh ginger, grated
1 tsp chilli oil
1 tsp sesame oil
1 tsp extra virgin olive oil
1 tbsp light soy sauce

First, salt the cucumber for the salad. Combine the cucumber and salt in a bowl, mix to coat well and set aside for 5 minutes. The salt will draw the excess moisture from the cucumber. Squeeze the cucumber over the sink to drain the excess liquid, pour out the liquid from the bowl and then place the cucumber back into the bowl.

Using a sharp knife, score the skin of the sea bass at 2.5cm intervals. Season both sides with a pinch of salt.

Heat the oil in a frying pan over a medium heat for 2–3 minutes, then gently place the fish in the pan skin side down and press down for 10 seconds to make sure the skin has full contact with the pan. Cook for 3–4 minutes, then flip and cook for a further 1 minute. Remove from the pan and leave to rest while you make everything else.

Place the pan back over a medium heat and add the butter, paprika and garlic. Cook for 1 minute, then add the soy sauce and sake (if using). Cook for a further 1 minute, then remove the pan from the heat and set aside.

Combine all the ingredients for the salad in a bowl and toss well.

Place the sea bass fillets on plates and spoon the paprika butter over the fillets. Finish with a generous handful of the salad.

TRIPLE GARLIC CRISPY CHICKEN WITH GREEN RICE AND SAUCE

PREP TIME 10 MINUTES · SERVES 2 · COOK TIME 20 MINUTES

Another insane crispy chicken dish to bless your kitchen! For me, this is the quintessential chicken recipe, featuring garlic, garlic and . . . you guessed it, more garlic! Influenced by secret Cantonese cooking techniques, the garlic is cooked in three different stages to bring out every single part of its garlicky essence, skins and all. It might as well be garlic with a side of chicken!

4 skin-on boneless chicken thighs
4 Tenderstem broccoli
2 spring onions, finely chopped
salt
cooked jasmine rice (see page 23), to serve

For the garlic sauce
10 garlic cloves, unpeeled
1 bird's eye chilli
1 banana shallot
3 tbsp vegetable oil
1 tbsp sesame oil
1 tbsp oyster sauce
1 tsp MSG
½ tsp granulated sugar
1 tbsp shop-bought fried shallots

For the green sauce
small bunch of mint
small bunch of coriander
1 spring onion
2 limes
2 tsp granulated sugar
1 tbsp fish sauce

First, make the garlic sauce. Put the garlic cloves, chilli and shallot into a food processor and blend until fine. Heat the vegetable oil in a small saucepan over a medium heat for 1–2 minutes, then add a third of the garlic mixture and cook for 1 minute. Add another third and cook for a further 1 minute, then add the last third, stir for a minute and remove from the heat. Add the sesame oil, oyster sauce, MSG and sugar. Stir to combine, scrape into a bowl and set aside.

For the green sauce, put all the ingredients into a food processor and blend until very smooth. Scrape into a bowl and set aside.

Pat the skin of the chicken dry with kitchen paper, then season both sides with salt. Place the chicken skin side down in a cold frying pan and turn the heat to medium. Cook for 7 minutes, then flip over and cook for a further 3 minutes. Remove from the pan, leaving the fat in the pan, and leave to rest while you cook the broccoli.

Put the broccoli into the same pan over a medium-high heat, season with a pinch of salt and fry for 3–4 minutes, flipping occasionally. Transfer to a food processor and blend until chunky, then combine the broccoli with the rice, add the spring onions and fold in.

Slice the chicken into 2–3cm thick pieces. Divide the rice between shallow plates, then add two sliced chicken thighs to each plate and generously spoon over the garlic sauce. Drizzle with the green sauce and finish with a generous sprinkling of fried shallots.

CHICKEN AND MUSHROOM LETTUCE CUPS

PREP TIME 20 MINUTES
SERVES 2
COOK TIME 25 MINUTES

A healthy, vegetable-packed minced chicken stir-fry, piled into a lettuce leaf, wrapped like a taco and then doused in a sweet hoisin sauce with tangy pickled onions. With plenty of herbs, chilli and garlic, these are light but filling, perfect for summer nights with your friends. It's a great sharing dish or starter, but so good you might not want to share!

2 iceberg lettuces
4 tbsp vegetable oil
1 banana shallot, thinly sliced
2 garlic cloves, very finely chopped
1 red chilli, finely chopped
500g minced chicken
150g asparagus, thinly sliced
½ carrot, finely diced
50g shiitake mushrooms (or chestnut mushrooms or other mushrooms of your choice), finely diced
2 tbsp oyster sauce
2 tsp fish sauce
1 tbsp light soy sauce
1 tsp granulated sugar
150ml chicken stock or water
2 tsp cornflour mixed with 2 tsp water, or as needed
small bunch of mint, thinly sliced
small bunch of coriander, thinly sliced
2 tbsp roasted peanuts, roughly chopped
2 tbsp shop-bought fried shallots

(Ingredients continue overleaf)

With the core facing down, slam the iceberg lettuces onto a surface a few times. Flip upside down and pull the cores out with your fingers. Run the lettuces under water, making sure the water gets in between every leaf. Gently separate all the leaves. Stack the leaves on top of one another and slice down the middle in half. Set aside.

Next, make the pickled red onions. Put the red onion and star anise into a bowl. Put the rice vinegar, water, salt and sugar into a saucepan over a high heat and stir to dissolve. Once simmering, remove from the heat and pour over the onion. Set aside.

Now make the sauce. Put the spring onion, chilli powder, sesame seeds, salt, sugar and MSG into a bowl. Heat the oil in a small saucepan over a high for 1–2 minutes, or until almost smoking. Pour the oil over the aromatics and stir to combine. Add the hoisin sauce, soy sauce, fish sauce and lime zest and juice. Mix to combine, then set aside.

Heat a large dry frying pan or wok over a high heat for 1–2 minutes, then add the oil. Add the shallots and fry for 2–3 minutes, or until they start to turn golden. Next, add the garlic and chilli and fry for a further 30 seconds. Add the minced chicken and use a wooden spoon to break up the meat. Fry for 3–4 minutes, or until browned. Now add the asparagus, carrot and mushrooms and fry for a further 2–3 minutes.

(Recipe continues overleaf)

For the pickled red onions
1 red onion, thinly sliced
1 star anise
175ml rice vinegar
55ml water
1 tsp salt
1 tbsp granulated sugar

For the sauce
1 spring onion, thinly sliced
2 tsp chilli powder
1 tbsp sesame seeds
½ tsp salt
½ tsp granulated sugar
½ tsp MSG
2 tbsp vegetable oil
5 tbsp hoisin sauce
1 tbsp light soy sauce
1 tsp fish sauce
zest and juice of 1 lime

Add the oyster sauce, fish sauce, soy sauce, sugar and chicken stock or water. Mix to combine. Slowly pour in the cornflour slurry while stirring. The sauce should coat the meat and not be runny. Add more slurry if it's too thin. Remove from the heat and pour into a bowl.

Drain the red onions and place them in a small bowl or on a plate. Place the lettuce leaves on the side of a large serving plate. Spoon the chicken mixture onto the plate, next to the lettuce. Sprinkle with the mint, coriander, chopped peanuts and fried shallots.

To eat, spoon the meat into a lettuce leaf, add a spoonful of sauce and a few pickled onions, then wrap it up and enjoy.

MISO BAKED SALMON WITH GRILLED SPRING ONIONS

PREP TIME 10 MINUTES
SERVES 2
COOK TIME 15 MINUTES

Miso-baked fish is one of the treats and treasures of this world, but it usually takes days to prepare and marinate. This recipe achieves the umami explosion we all crave, in less time. The miso sauce can be used on any type of protein, but my preference is salmon. Whole spring onions, flash-fried with ginger and chilli and drizzled with lemon juice and zest, help to balance the rich and flavourful fish.

2 tbsp miso paste
4 tbsp mirin
2 tbsp light brown soft sugar
6 spring onions, trimmed
1 tbsp olive oil
1 tsp chilli flakes
zest and juice of 1 lemon, plus extra wedges to serve
1 thumb-sized piece of fresh ginger, grated
pinch of salt
2 x 200g salmon fillets
1 tbsp unsalted butter
large handful of chives, finely chopped

Preheat the oven to 200°C/180°C fan/gas mark 6 and line a baking tray with foil.

Combine the miso paste, mirin and brown sugar in a bowl and whisk thoroughly.

Put the spring onions onto a plate and toss with the olive oil, chilli flakes, lemon zest, ginger and salt.

Pat the salmon fillets dry using kitchen paper. Place the fillets on the prepared baking tray and brush them with a light coating of the miso mixture, reserving the rest. Bake in the oven for 12 minutes, then remove and leave to rest for 5 minutes.

Meanwhile, heat a large frying pan over a high heat for about 3 minutes. Add the spring onions and cook for 2–3 minutes on each side. They should be slightly charred and golden. Remove from the pan and drizzle with a squeeze of lemon.

In the same pan over a high heat, melt the butter. Pour in the remaining miso mixture, add half the chives and swirl the pan for 20–30 seconds. Set aside in a bowl.

Put the salmon on plates and spoon over the miso sauce. Sprinkle with the remaining chives. Add the charred spring onions to the side. Serve with a wedge of lemon.

GRILLED CUMIN CHICKEN AND HERB CAESAR SALAD

An Asian twist on a summer classic. Bashed chicken breasts are coated in freshly ground cumin and Sichuan peppercorns, slapped on the griddle pan until those beautiful char marks appear, and served with Caesar salad dressed with lime, chives and soy. Of course the usual suspects are there too . . . plenty of crunchy lettuce, anchovies and croutons.

2 chicken breasts
1 tbsp cumin seeds, toasted and ground
1 tsp Sichuan peppercorns, toasted and ground
1 tsp salt
1 tsp freshly ground black pepper
pinch of MSG (optional)
1 tbsp olive oil
6 anchovies in oil
small bunch of coriander, leaves picked
1 tbsp chilli oil
1 lime, cut into wedges

For the croutons
1 tbsp unsalted butter
2 slices of white bread (or any bread), cut into 2.5cm cubes
salt and freshly ground black pepper

For the salad
2 tbsp mayonnaise
1 tsp Worcestershire sauce
1 tsp Tabasco
1 tsp Dijon mustard
1 tbsp light soy sauce
zest and juice of 1 lime
small bunch of chives, thinly sliced
50g Parmesan, grated, plus extra to serve
pinch of salt
1 romaine lettuce, leaves separated

First, make the croutons. Melt the butter in a small frying pan over a medium heat, then add the cubes of bread and toast for 5 minutes, stirring and flipping regularly until evenly toasted and golden brown. Transfer to a plate and season with salt and pepper. Set aside to cool.

Place a chicken breast on one side of a piece of baking paper, fold the rest of the paper over the top and bash the chicken with a rolling pin until it is 2cm thick. Repeat with the remaining breast.

In a small bowl, mix together the spices, salt, black pepper, MSG (if using) and olive oil to form a paste. Spoon the paste over the chicken breasts and rub in thoroughly.

Heat a dry griddle pan over a high heat for about 3 minutes, or until smoking. Place the chicken breasts in the pan and press down with your fingers. Cook for 3–4 minutes on each side, or until nicely charred. Remove the chicken from the pan and leave to rest for 5 minutes.

Meanwhile, combine all the ingredients for the salad except the lettuce in a large bowl and stir well to combine. Add the lettuce leaves and toss to coat every leaf in the dressing.

Slice the chicken breasts into 2–3cm pieces. Arrange the chicken breasts in fans on a plate, then add the salad, followed by a grating of Parmesan. Sprinkle the croutons on top and drape the anchovy fillets on top of the leaves. Scatter a small handful of coriander over the plate, drizzle with chilli oil and finish with a wedge of lime.

LEMONGRASS CHICKEN WITH HERB SALAD

PLUS MARINATING TIME

These turmeric and lemongrass chicken thighs are served with jammy burnt lime wedges and a super-earthy herb salad. Ideally you would cook the chicken on a charcoal barbecue to give it a smoky aroma and thick grill marks, but the method below offers options for a griddle pan or a grill so you can make it even on rainy days. Perfect for beer season with a bowl of white rice, or add the chicken to anything from salads to wraps!

2 lemongrass sticks, bottom halves finely chopped
½ banana shallot, finely chopped
1 tsp ground turmeric
1 tbsp oyster sauce
2 tsp fish sauce
2 tsp light soy sauce
1 tsp dark soy sauce
1 tsp freshly ground black pepper
1 tsp granulated sugar
pinch of MSG
pinch of salt
1 tbsp vegetable oil
6 skin-on boneless chicken thighs
1 lime, halved

For the herb salad
small bunch of coriander, roughly chopped
small bunch of mint, leaves picked
small bunch of chives, roughly chopped
small bunch of Thai basil, leaves picked
½ banana shallot, thinly sliced

For the dressing
1 tbsp sesame seeds
2 tsp extra virgin olive oil
zest of 1 lime
juice of ⅓ lime
pinch of MSG
pinch of salt

Combine all the ingredients except the chicken and lime in a bowl and stir until the sugar has dissolved. Place the chicken in the bowl and coat evenly in the marinade, making sure to get into all the nooks and crannies. Cover with cling film and set aside in the fridge to marinate for at least 30 minutes or, even better, overnight.

Meanwhile, prepare the salad. Combine all the salad ingredients in a bowl and toss to combine. In a separate small bowl, combine the ingredients for the dressing and whisk well.

To cook the chicken in a griddle pan
Heat a dry griddle pan over a high heat for 3 minutes, or until smoking. Place the chicken thighs in the pan flesh side down. Using your fingers, gently press down to make sure the chicken has enough contact with the pan. Cook for 3–4 minutes, then flip over and cook for a further 3–4 minutes. Remove the chicken from the pan and allow it to rest for 5 minutes.

Place the halved lime in the pan flesh side down and cook for 2–3 minutes, or until the flesh is charred.

To cook the chicken under the grill
Preheat the grill on high for 5 minutes. Place the chicken skin side down on a wire rack set over a baking tray. Cook under the grill for 4–5 minutes, then flip and cook for a further 3 minutes, or until the skin has charred but is not burnt. Remove from the oven and leave to rest for 5 minutes.

Place the halved lime in a small, dry frying pan flesh side down and cook over a high heat for 2–3 minutes, or until the flesh is charred.

Slice the chicken into 2–3cm pieces. Pour the dressing over the salad and toss thoroughly. Place the chicken thighs on plates, followed by a generous handful of salad. Garnish with the burnt lime.

GINGER AND ONION RIB-EYE STEAK

This restaurant-quality dish is perfect for date nights as it is sure to impress that special someone in your life. Inspired by Japanese hibachi restaurants, it features perfectly cooked steak on a bed of addictive and punchy ginger and onion sauce, which is then topped with an umami miso butter and cress to cut through the richness. You do not want to miss this one. Serve with a bowl of steaming rice. This feeds two, but if you're having a long day, just have it to yourself!

400g rib-eye steak
pinch of salt
few cracks of black pepper
2 tbsp vegetable oil
1 tbsp miso paste
1 tbsp mirin (or water)
small bunch of chives, thinly sliced
1 tbsp unsalted butter
20g cress
cooked jasmine rice (see page 23), to serve

For the ginger and onion sauce
1 onion, roughly chopped
1 thumb-sized piece of fresh ginger, roughly chopped
zest and juice of 1 lime
4 tbsp light soy sauce
5 tbsp rice vinegar
1 tbsp tomato ketchup
2 tsp granulated sugar

Start by making the ginger and onion sauce. Combine all the ingredients in a food processor and blend for 45 seconds – you want it to have small chunks rather than be a smooth paste. Transfer to a bowl and set aside. Tip: the longer this sauce sits, the better the flavour.

Season the steak with the salt and pepper on both sides.

Heat a dry frying pan over a high heat for 1–2 minutes, then pour in the oil and gently add the steak. Fry for 1–2 minutes on each side for medium-rare, or cook to your preference. Remove the steak and set aside on a plate or board to rest while you make the miso butter.

Combine the miso paste, mirin and chives in a bowl and whisk until combined.

Put the butter into the pan you cooked the steak in and place over a medium heat. Once the butter has melted, add the miso mixture and cook for 30 seconds, or until bubbling. Remove from the heat and set aside until needed.

Slice the steak into 1–2cm strips, against the grain. Pour the ginger and onion sauce onto a lipped serving plate and shake the plate to cover it with the sauce. Place the sliced steak on top, then spoon over the miso butter. Garnish with the cress and a wedge of lime, then serve with rice.

FEEDING A CROWD?

DISHES TO SHARE

Sometimes the stress of hosting can be a lot. Going far and beyond to put on a spread for your guests can put people off, especially with the amount of ingredients used in most recipes – it's as if a tornado hit your kitchen! These recipes not only provide a stress-free way to impress, but also make the clean-up easier by using just a few pots and pans. The recipes that serve two can easily be doubled (or tripled) depending on how many people you're cooking for.

CRISPY GARLIC PORK BELLY BITES

Easy double-fried pork belly bites marinated in soy and fish sauce and cooked until crispy sound pretty good already, but they're not the star of the show. The REAL star is the crispy garlic breadcrumbs that are piled on top by the bucketload. When they come together, it's a crispy, garlicky, spicy and salty sensation that goes perfect with a bowl of steaming rice – or it's amazing just eaten as it is as a snack. These are to me what buffalo wings are to Americans – a proper sports bar kind of food.

800g pork belly, skin removed and sliced into 2.5cm chunks
1 tbsp light soy sauce
1 tbsp dark soy sauce
1 tbsp fish sauce
1 tbsp granulated sugar
1 tbsp freshly ground black pepper
1 tbsp finely chopped fresh ginger
3 tbsp plain flour
3 tbsp cornflour
750ml vegetable oil, or as needed
small bunch of coriander, thinly sliced
2 limes, cut into wedges

For the garlic breadcrumbs
20 garlic cloves, very finely chopped or pulsed in a blender with the skins on
150g dried breadcrumbs
1 tsp salt
1 tsp granulated sugar
1 tsp MSG
1 tbsp vegetable oil
2 red chillies, thinly sliced
4 spring onions, thinly sliced
½ onion, diced

Put the pork belly into a bowl with the light and dark soy sauce, fish sauce, sugar, black pepper and ginger. Mix thoroughly, then set aside to marinate for 10 minutes.

In a large bowl, combine the flour and cornflour, then add the marinated pork belly. Toss to coat, ensuring every surface is well covered.

Heat 2.5–5cm oil in a large, deep saucepan over a medium heat until it reaches 170°C. To test the oil, hold a chopstick in the pan. If bubbles rapidly form around the chopstick, the oil is ready. Gently lower half the pork into the oil and fry for 2–3 minutes until sealed but not fully browned (cooking it in two batches avoids crowding the pan and lowering the heat of the oil), then remove from the oil with a slotted spoon and repeat with the remaining pork.

Let the pork cool for 5 minutes, or until cool to the touch. Meanwhile, increase the heat to medium-high and bring the oil up to 190°C. Add half the cooled pork belly to the oil and fry for 60–90 seconds, or until golden. Remove with a slotted spoon and place on kitchen paper to remove any excess oil. Repeat with the remaining pork, then lower the heat to medium-low.

Combine the garlic and breadcrumbs in a large bowl, then add to the hot oil and stir. Cook for 1 minute, then remove from the heat and allow to cook for a further 1–2 minutes, or until golden brown. Remove the garlic breadcrumbs with a slotted spoon and place back into the bowl. Sprinkle with half the salt, MSG and sugar, then toss to combine.

Heat the tablespoon of vegetable oil in a frying pan over a high heat. Add the chillies, spring onions and diced onion along with the remaining salt, sugar and MSG. Stir-fry for 1 minute, then add to the bowl of garlic breadcrumbs.

Place the pork belly bites onto a large platter. Generously heap the garlic breadcrumbs on top, then sprinkle with the coriander and serve with the wedges of lime.

FEEDING A CROWD? DISHES TO SHARE

CREAM CHEESE SALMON SUSHI TACOS

PREP TIME 25 MINUTES
SERVES 4
COOK TIME 25 MINUTES

Here's one that will have your friends obsessed, and probably keep them nagging you to cook it over and over . . . or you could just tell them to buy this book! Rice is layered with flaked salmon, Japanese mayo and more before being baked in the oven to caramelise the mayo until golden brown, then finished with spring onions, sriracha and sesame seeds. Nori seaweed serves as the taco 'shells' – just grab a spoonful of rice and a slice of avocado, wrap and enjoy!

1 tbsp olive oil
4 x 120g skinless salmon fillets
200g crabsticks, shredded
4 spring onions, thinly sliced
175g cream cheese
2 tbsp Japanese mayonnaise, such as Kewpie
3 tbsp sriracha
2 tbsp light soy sauce
1 tsp MSG
pinch of salt
1 tsp freshly ground black pepper
zest and juice of 1 lemon
1 tsp granulated sugar
1 tbsp sesame oil

For the rice
450g cooked Japanese short-grain rice (see page 23)
150ml shop-bought sushi seasoning (recommended)
or
55ml rice vinegar
25ml mirin
40g granulated sugar
25g salt

For the topping
3 tbsp sriracha
handful of coriander
3 tbsp Japanese mayonnaise, such as Kewpie
3 tbsp sesame seeds
handful of chives, thinly sliced

To serve
8 sheets of nori seaweed, cut into quarters
3 avocados, sliced
8 tbsp light soy sauce
1 tbsp wasabi

First, prepare the rice. Put the freshly cooked rice into a large, shallow oven dish. If you're making your own sushi seasoning, combine the ingredients in a bowl and stir until the sugar and salt have dissolved. Pour the sushi seasoning over the rice and then use a rice paddle or wooden spoon to gently mix it in without breaking the rice until all the grains have been coated and the seasoning has soaked in. This should take 2–4 minutes. Gently spread out the rice to cover the entire surface of the dish, but do not pack too tightly.

Preheat the oven to 200°C/180°C fan/gas mark 6.

Heat the olive oil in a frying pan over medium heat for 1–2 minutes, then add the salmon fillets and cook for 3 minutes on each side. Transfer to a plate and use your fingers to shred the fish into large flakes.

Put all the remaining ingredients for the salmon into a large bowl and mix thoroughly to combine. Add the flaked salmon and gently fold through the mixture, preserving the flakes. Spoon the mixture over the rice to cover it completely.

Bake on the middle shelf of the oven for 10 minutes, then turn the oven to the grill setting and cook for a further 2–3 minutes, or until golden brown. Remove and leave to rest for 5–10 minutes until slightly cooled.

Once cooled, add the topping. Drizzle with the sriracha from edge to edge, in a zig-zag. Sprinkle the coriander on top and add small dollops of mayonnaise around the dish. Finally, sprinkle with the sesame seeds and chives.

To serve, place the dish in the middle of the table along with the nori squares, sliced avocado and soy sauce and wasabi in small bowls.

To eat, grab a sheet of nori and add a spoonful of rice and salmon followed by a slice of avocado. Fold it over like a taco, and dip it into the soy and wasabi like you would sushi.

SPICY GREEN BEAN AND TOFU STEW v

PREP TIME 15 MINUTES
SERVES 4
COOK TIME 20 MINUTES

A heartwarming one-pot dish filled with herbs, vegetables and spice, this is one to make on a cosy night in. I use two types of tofu here for added texture, but if you can only get one, that's fine. Similar to mapo tofu but without the meat, I love adding this saucy stew to fresh egg noodles along with heaps of coriander and cucumber. Of course, if you want, this also goes well with steamed rice, but what beats a slurpy noodle?

2 tbsp vegetable oil
3 garlic cloves, finely chopped
2cm piece of fresh ginger, finely chopped
1 bird's eye chilli, finely chopped
1 celery stick, diced
200g green beans, thinly sliced
2 tbsp doubanjiang (fermented chilli bean paste)
1 tbsp light soy sauce
1 tsp granulated sugar
100g fried tofu puffs, cut in half (optional)
250ml vegetable or chicken stock
1½ tbsp cornflour mixed with 1½ tbsp water
2 tbsp chilli oil
1 tsp sesame oil
400g medium-soft tofu, cut into 2–3cm cubes
1 spring onion, thinly sliced on the diagonal

To serve
4 x 150g bundles of fresh egg noodles (or instant noodles or udon)
2 tbsp sesame seeds, toasted
½ cucumber, cut into matchsticks
small bunch of coriander, finely chopped

Heat the vegetable oil in a wok or large frying pan over a high heat for about 1 minute, then add the garlic, ginger and chilli and stir-fry for 1 minute. Add the celery, green beans, doubanjiang, light soy sauce and sugar and stir-fry for a further 1–2 minutes, then add the tofu puffs and give it a stir to coat it in the sauce before finally pouring in the stock.

Bring everything to the boil and cook for 1–2 minutes, then reduce the heat to low and slowly pour in the cornstarch slurry while stirring. Increase the heat to medium again and simmer gently for 1–2 minutes until the sauce starts to thicken.

Once it has started to thicken, reduce the heat back to low and add the chilli oil, sesame oil and medium-soft tofu. Stir very gently to coat the tofu in the sauce, then simmer for 3 minutes. Finally, add the spring onions and give it a final stir. Remove from the heat.

Bring a saucepan of water to the boil and cook the noodles for 1 minute less than the time stated on the packet, then drain and immediately divide between bowls. Ladle over a generous amount of the stew – it should completely cover the noodles – then add a sprinkle of sesame seeds, cucumber and coriander. Mix thoroughly and consume immediately – if you leave the noodles sitting for too long, they'll clump up.

CORIANDER AND LIME BUTTER DRUMSTICKS WITH CELERY AND CORIANDER SALAD

PREP TIME 5 MINUTES · SERVES 4 · COOK TIME 50 MINUTES

These crispy oven-cooked chicken drumsticks tossed in the most addictive herby garlic butter you can imagine always remind me of summer trips away with friends. A giant plate of these, paired with a celery and coriander salad, beer and good company, makes for one hell of an evening. Tip: if you can, grill them on a barbecue!

1.5kg chicken drumsticks
1 tsp salt
1 tbsp light soy sauce
1 tbsp freshly ground black pepper
3 tbsp unsalted butter
5 garlic cloves, very finely chopped
zest and juice of 2 limes
1 tbsp miso paste
1 tbsp sesame seeds
1 tbsp chilli powder, or to taste
small bunch of mint, thinly sliced
small bunch of coriander, thinly sliced
small bunch of chives, thinly sliced

For the umami salt
1 tbsp salt
1 tbsp MSG
1 tbsp granulated sugar

For the celery and coriander salad
1 red onion, thinly sliced
2 celery sticks, sliced diagonally into 1–2cm strips
small bunch of coriander, roughly chopped
zest and juice of 1 lime
pinch of salt
1 tbsp extra virgin olive oil

Preheat the oven to 200°C/180°C fan/gas mark 6.

In a large bowl, toss the chicken with the salt, soy sauce and black pepper. Mix well to coat. Place the chicken on a wire rack set over a baking tray, or line the baking tray with foil. Cook in the oven for 40 minutes, flipping halfway through. Once cooked, remove from the oven and leave to rest for 5 minutes.

Meanwhile, combine all the ingredients for the umami salt in a small bowl.

Put the butter, garlic, lime zest, miso paste, sesame seeds and chilli powder into a small saucepan over a medium heat and whisk for 2–3 minutes until the butter has melted and started to foam and the miso paste has combined. Remove from the heat and add the lime juice.

Next, prepare the salad. Put the onion, celery and coriander into a bowl. Just before serving, add the lime zest and juice, salt and oil. Toss to combine.

Place the cooked chicken drumsticks into a large bowl. Sprinkle over the umami salt and toss until evenly covered, then add the mint, coriander and chives. Pour the miso garlic butter into the bowl and toss thoroughly, covering the chicken.

Place the chicken onto a large plate, then arrange the salad on the side. Have a bite of chicken and chase with a pinch of the salad.

FEEDING A CROWD? DISHES TO SHARE

SWEET BRAISED CHICKEN AND MUSHROOM RICE

PREP TIME 20 MINUTES
SERVES 4
COOK TIME 55 MINUTES

The smell of a giant pot of braised chicken and mushrooms is so good I could bathe in it . . . wait, I meant eat it! You get the gist. I'm using a classic Chinese braising liquid, which imparts its umami-ness into all the ingredients as they slow-cook until tender. It's finished with a splash of scorching oil to get all the good stuff out of the aromatics that are piled on top. As always, eat with a bowl of white rice . . . sorry not sorry, I am Asian, after all!

2 tbsp vegetable oil
4 garlic cloves, finely chopped
1 banana shallot, finely chopped
1 thumb-sized piece of fresh ginger, finely chopped
8 skinless and boneless chicken thighs, cut into 2–3cm pieces
8 dried shiitake mushrooms, soaked in boiling water for 1 hour, then stems removed and cut in half (or fresh shiitake, not soaked)
200g fried tofu puffs (optional)
600ml chicken stock
1 star anise
1 cinnamon stick
3 tbsp light soy sauce
3 tbsp dark soy sauce
2 tbsp oyster sauce
2 tbsp hoisin sauce
40g rock sugar
2 sweetcorn cobs
2–3 tbsp cornflour mixed with 2–3 tbsp water
cooked jasmine rice (see page 23), to serve

For the scorched aromatics
1 tbsp chilli flakes
1 tbsp sesame seeds
small bunch of coriander, roughly chopped
small bunch of chives, cut into thirds
1 garlic clove, finely chopped
2 tbsp vegetable oil

Heat the oil in a large casserole dish or saucepan (or a claypot if you have one) over a high heat for 1–2 minutes, then add the garlic, shallot and ginger. Fry for 1–2 minutes, or until slightly coloured. Add the chicken, mushrooms and tofu and stir-fry for a further 1–2 minutes, then pour in the chicken stock. Finally, add the star anise, cinnamon stick, light and dark soy sauce, oyster sauce, hoisin sauce and rock sugar. Stir to combine, then bring to the boil. Once boiling, cover and reduce the heat to low. Cook for 45 minutes, stirring halfway through.

Meanwhile, heat a dry frying pan over a high heat. Add the sweetcorn and char for about 4–5 minutes on each side until blackened all over. Remove and leave to cool. Tip: if you have a blowtorch, you can use this instead as it will scorch the skin in seconds. Once cooled, hold the cob on its end and run the knife down close to the core to slice off clusters of kernels.

After the chicken has braised, remove the lid and reduce the heat to the lowest setting. Slowly pour the cornflour slurry into the pan while stirring. The consistency should be slightly thick and glossy. You might not need all of the slurry. If it's too thick, add a splash of water.

Arrange the sweetcorn around the dish, then pile the chilli flakes, sesame seeds, coriander, chives and garlic for the scorched aromatics in the middle. Heat the vegetable oil in a small pan over a high heat until smoking, then pour on top. Enjoy with rice.

POACHED CHICKEN GRAVY RICE

Think cheap Chinese takeaway with this dish: meat and a heap of gravy on rice, but all done at home, fuss-free and packed with comforting flavour! Check the seasoning after adding the cornflour slurry to the sauce as the reduction of the sauce might vary due to different hobs or sizes of pans – add more salt and light soy sauce if necessary.

225g jasmine rice
1 thumb-sized piece of fresh ginger
5 garlic cloves, unpeeled
1 tbsp vegetable oil
2 spring onions
340ml chicken stock
150g rock sugar
4 skin-on boneless chicken thighs
1 star anise
1 cinnamon stick
500ml water
5 tbsp light soy sauce, plus extra as needed
5 tbsp dark soy sauce
3 tbsp cornflour mixed with 3 tbsp water
salt

To serve
1 spring onion, cut into thin matchsticks and placed in ice-cold water
small bunch of coriander, sliced into 5cm pieces and placed in ice-cold water

Put the rice into a bowl and cover with cold water. Rinse the rice and then pour out the water. Repeat this twice, or until the water is clear, then drain.

Cut 2 slices from the ginger and cut them into matchsticks. Finely chop 2 of the garlic cloves.

Heat a saucepan over a medium heat and add the oil. Add the chopped garlic, ginger matchsticks and one of the spring onions and stir-fry for 1 minute. Add the rice, a pinch of salt and chicken stock. Stir once to combine, then cover, increase the heat to high and bring to the boil. As soon as the water is at a rolling boil, reduce the heat to the lowest setting. Cook for 18 minutes without removing the lid. After this time, remove the pan from the heat and set aside, covered, until you're ready to serve.

Put the rock sugar and a splash of water into a separate saucepan over a medium heat and stir thoroughly for about 2 minutes to dissolve the sugar. Once dissolved, keep stirring – after about 5 minutes, the sugar will slowly caramelise and turn golden brown. Next, add the chicken thighs, the remaining spring onions, the remaining garlic cloves (unpeeled), the remaining ginger (whole), the star anise, cinnamon stick, water, a big pinch of salt and the light and dark soy sauce. Cover, increase the heat to high and bring to a rolling boil, then turn the heat down to low and cook for 25 minutes.

After 25 minutes, remove the chicken from the liquid and discard all the aromatics. Keep the heat on low. Slowly pour in the cornflour and water slurry while stirring. The sauce should be smooth with the consistency of gravy. If it's too thin, add a bit more, if it's too thick add a splash of water. Taste and check the seasoning, adding a pinch of salt and more light soy sauce if needed.

Slice the chicken into strips. Divide the rice between shallow plates, then place the chicken on top and drizzle with a generous amount of gravy. Add the spring onion and coriander garnish. Enjoy!

CRISPY NOODLES WITH PRAWN, ASPARAGUS AND MUSHROOM SAUCE

A home-made alternative to the world-famous classic Chinese restaurant dish, these addictive crispy noodles bring absolutely everything you crave from a takeaway: namely, texture and heaps of sauce. Think of it like a pancake – one side's crispy, one side's soft. We all know which side is worth fighting for! The technique is to spread the noodles out in the pan as much as possible, as this will ensure you're maximising the crunchy deliciousness. Take your time with this one – low and slow equals extra crispy noodles!

2 packets of instant noodles (any type)
6 tbsp vegetable oil
150g raw peeled king prawns (or firm tofu, cut into 3cm cubes)
6 asparagus tips
4 mushrooms (preferably shiitake), sliced
¼ carrot, cut into matchsticks
6 baby corn
handful of mangetout
200ml vegetable or chicken stock
½ tbsp light soy sauce
1 tbsp oyster sauce
1 tsp granulated sugar
dash of ground white pepper
1 tbsp cornflour
75ml cold water
1 tsp sesame oil
handful of coriander
1 spring onion, thinly sliced
1 tbsp chilli oil

Bring a saucepan of water to the boil and cook the noodles according to the packet instructions (without adding the flavouring sachets), then drain and set aside.

Heat a wok or large frying pan over a medium heat. Add 4 tablespoons of the oil, then add the cooked instant noodles and spread them out against the bottom of the pan, forming a round pancake shape. Shake the pan occasionally to ensure the bottom doesn't burn. Once the bottom is nicely browned and crispy, around 5 minutes, flip the noodles onto a plate, brown side up.

Put the pan back on the stove, still over a medium heat, and add 2 tablespoons oil. Add the prawns/tofu, asparagus, mushrooms, baby corn, mangetout and carrots, then stir-fry for around 3 mins. Add the chicken stock, light soy sauce, oyster sauce, sugar and white pepper. Stir to combine and bring to the boil. Once boiling, mix the cornstarch and cold water to make a slurry. Turn the heat to low and slowly drizzle in the slurry while stirring. The sauce should thicken – if it's too thin, add more slurry; if too thick, add a splash of water. Add in the sesame oil and cook for 1 minute, then turn off the heat.

Add the noodles to a large plate, crispy side up. Pour the sauce on top of the noodles. Add the spring onion and coriander, drizzle with your favourite chilli oil and enjoy!

FEEDING A CROWD? DISHES TO SHARE

CHICKEN AND MUSHROOM CLAYPOT RICE

PREP TIME 15 MINUTES
SERVES 4
COOK TIME 25 MINUTES

My go-to dish to feed a crowd! This one is super simple, requires just one pot, has huge flavour and is cooked in under 30 minutes. Bite-sized chicken pieces and meaty mushrooms are covered in a sea of spring onions and chives, making it the perfect well-rounded and filling stress-free meal. The glue that holds this together is the sizzling ginger and spring onion sauce that you often find with Chinese chicken and roast meats – this and some chilli oil equals heaven.

600g jasmine rice
8 skinless and boneless chicken thighs, cut into bite-sized pieces
1 tsp salt
1 tsp MSG
2 tbsp light soy sauce
1 tbsp cornflour
½ tbsp water
650ml chicken stock
300g Tenderstem broccoli, sliced into 1cm pieces
2 Chinese sausages, sliced into 1cm pieces (optional)
120g shiitake mushrooms, destemmed and sliced
2 tbsp sesame seeds
2 spring onions, thinly sliced
large bunch of chives, thinly sliced

For the sweet soy sauce
4 tbsp light soy sauce
4 tbsp dark soy sauce
1 tbsp granulated sugar
1 tsp MSG
3 tbsp sesame oil
pinch of salt

For the ginger sauce
2 spring onions, very finely chopped
1 thumb sized piece of fresh ginger, very finely chopped
1 tsp salt
1 tsp MSG
3 tbsp vegetable oil

Put the rice into a bowl and cover with cold water. Rinse the rice and then pour out the water. Repeat this twice, or until the water is clear, then drain.

Put the chicken pieces into a bowl and add the salt, MSG, soy sauce, cornflour and water. Mix thoroughly until the chicken is fully coated.

Heat a large, heavy-based saucepan over a high heat for about 1 minute, then pour in the drained rice and add the chicken stock. Cover with a lid and bring to the boil. Once boiling, remove the lid and cover the surface with the broccoli, Chinese sausage, chicken and mushrooms, in that order. Make sure to spread out the ingredients, especially the chicken, to ensure even cooking – spread the ingredients right to the edge of the pan. Put the lid back on and reduce the heat to the lowest setting. Cook for 18 minutes. Meanwhile, make the sweet soy sauce and ginger sauce.

Combine all the ingredients for the sweet soy sauce in a bowl and stir until the sugar has dissolved, then set aside.

To make the ginger sauce, put the spring onions and ginger into a bowl with the salt and MSG. Heat the oil in a small saucepan over a high heat for 1–2 minutes, or until almost smoking. Gently pour the oil into the bowl and stir to combine.

Once the rice is cooked, remove the pan from the heat and, if you have time, leave to rest with the lid on for 8–10 minutes.

When you're ready to serve, sprinkle over the sesame seeds, sliced spring onions and chives. Evenly pour over the sweet soy sauce, making sure to cover the majority of rice. Do the same with the ginger sauce. Put the lid back on and let it rest for 5 minutes. Once rested, give the rice a stir before serving.

NOTE The chicken in this dish is super tender thanks to a traditional Chinese technique called velveting, which involves marinating the meat with cornflour.

SPICY BRAISED PORK SAUCY NOODLES

Almost like an East Asian spaghetti Bolognese . . . well, the Chinese did invent pasta, so I guess this is actually the OG (sorry, Italians!). It's a super-simple one-pot dish consisting of a spicy braised minced meat sauce full of umami that is ladled on top of piping hot noodles. Give it a stir and get slurping! This sauce works with udon noodles too if you prefer.

3 tbsp vegetable oil
3 garlic cloves, very finely chopped
1 onion, diced
1 red chilli, finely chopped
400g minced pork
1 tbsp doubanjiang (fermented chilli bean paste) or gochujang paste
800ml water
1 tbsp oyster sauce
1 tbsp light soy sauce
3 tbsp dark soy sauce
1 tsp granulated sugar
1 tsp MSG (optional)
pinch of ground white pepper
200g green beans, finely chopped
1 tbsp cornflour mixed with 1 tbsp water
1 tsp sesame oil
4 x 120g bundles of fresh egg noodles (or instant noodles)
2 tbsp chilli oil (optional)
1 tbsp sesame seeds

Heat a heavy-based saucepan over a high heat for 1–2 minutes, then pour in the vegetable oil, followed by the garlic, onion and chilli. Fry for 1 minute, then add the minced pork and use a wooden spoon to break up and separate the meat. Fry for a further 3–5 minutes until the water has evaporated and the meat starts to brown.

Add the doubanjiang and stir to coat the meat for a minute or so. Next, add the water, oyster sauce, light and dark soy sauce, sugar, MSG and white pepper. Cover and bring to the boil. Once boiling, reduce the heat to medium-low and cook for 20 minutes.

After 20 minutes, add the green beans, stir and cover again, then cook for a further 20 minutes. If the meat starts to catch on the bottom, reduce the heat, and if it begins to look dry, add a splash of water.

Once the sauce has partially reduced, pour in the cornflour slurry while stirring. It should thicken. Finally, stir in the sesame oil and then remove from the heat

Bring a saucepan of water to the boil and cook the noodles according to the packet instructions, then drain and divide between bowls. Generously ladle the meat sauce on top. Drizzle over the chilli oil (if using) and sprinkle over the sesame seeds.

TENDER BRAISED LAMB WITH QUICK-PICKLED CHILLIES

PREP TIME 10 MINUTES
SERVES 2
COOK TIME 45 MINUTES

Similar to the famous Cantonese braised beef brisket or a British hotpot, this rich and saucy braised lamb pairs magically with the Chinese trinity of spices: cinnamon, star anise and ginger! It's an easy one-pot dish, slow-cooked to make the lamb fork-tender. Put the lid on, make a cuppa, turn on the telly and put your feet up. The secret to the wonderfully sweet and rich sauce is a traditional Chinese technique of melting sugar in water to create a caramel to sear the meat in. Pair it with a quick pickled chilli and steaming hot rice.

400g boneless lamb shoulder, diced
5 tbsp dark soy sauce
50g rock sugar
850ml water, plus extra as needed
1 tsp Chinese five-spice powder
1 thumb-sized piece of fresh ginger, smashed with a knife
8 garlic cloves, peeled but left whole
1 spring onion, cut into thirds
6 banana shallots, ends cut off but left whole
2 star anise
1 cinnamon stick
2 dried chillies (optional)
2 bay leaves
4 tbsp light soy sauce
1 tbsp cornflour mixed with 1 tbsp water, or as needed
large bunch of chives, thinly sliced
1 tbsp sesame seeds
cooked jasmine or Japanese short-grain rice (see page 23), to serve

For the quick-pickled chillies
2 tbsp rice vinegar
1 tsp granulated sugar
1 tsp salt
2 red chillies, sliced

First, make the quick-pickled chillies. Combine the vinegar, sugar and salt in a small bowl and stir until the sugar has dissolved. Submerge the chillies in the pickling liquid, then set aside for 30 minutes to pickle.

Next, put the lamb into a bowl with 1 tablespoon of the dark soy sauce. Mix to coat thoroughly, then set aside.

Put the rock sugar and 3 tablespoons of the water into a saucepan over a medium heat and slowly stir to dissolve. Keep stirring until the water has evaporated and continue until the sugar has caramelised to a deep brown colour – this should take 5–7 minutes. As soon as it has, add the lamb pieces and five-spice powder. Stir for 30 seconds to coat the lamb, then add the remaining water and stir for 1 minute until everything is combined. Add the ginger, garlic, spring onion, shallots, star anise, cinnamon stick, dried chillies (if using) and bay leaves. Put the lid on, increase the heat to high and bring to the boil. Once boiling, reduce the heat to medium-low and cook for 45 minutes. If the level of liquid drops below the lamb, add 50ml water.

Once the sauce has reduced but has not completely thickened, slowly pour the cornflour slurry into the pan while stirring. The consistency should be thick and glossy like a gravy – add more slurry if it's too thin. Remove from the heat.

Divide the rice between shallow bowls, place it on one side, then ladle the braised lamb on the other side. Generously sprinkle over the chives and sesame seeds, then finish with some of the quick-pickled chillies.

BRAISED MINCED BEEF WITH CRISPY FRIED LEEKS AND EGGS

PREP TIME 7 MINUTES
SERVES 4
COOK TIME 1 HOUR

As a child, I'd often come home to a pot of braised minced beef gravy that my mum had cooked. I'd grab a big bowl of rice from the rice cooker and ladle after ladle, drown it in sauce from the pot. It's a simple but comforting one-pot dish that just might become your next weekly staple . . . actually, it definitely will!

8 tbsp vegetable oil
4 garlic cloves, very finely chopped
1 thumb-sized piece of fresh ginger, very finely chopped
1 onion, finely diced
2 celery sticks, finely diced
500g minced beef
1 litre beef stock
2 tbsp light soy sauce
4 tbsp dark soy sauce
2 tbsp oyster sauce
1 tsp granulated sugar
1 tsp MSG (optional)
1 leek
pinch of salt
4 medium eggs
150g frozen peas
2 tbsp cornflour mixed with 2 tbsp water
2 tbsp sesame seeds
small bunch of coriander, thinly sliced
4 tsp chilli oil
cooked jasmine rice (see page 23), to serve

Heat 2 tablespoons of the oil in a heavy-based saucepan over a high heat for 1–2 minutes, then add the garlic and ginger and fry for 30 seconds before adding the onion and celery. Fry for 2–3 minutes, then add the minced beef and use a wooden spoon to break it up into small pieces. Cook for 6–8 minutes until the liquid has evaporated and the meat has browned, then add the stock, light and dark soy sauce, oyster sauce, sugar and MSG (if using). Bring to the boil, then reduce the heat to low, cover and cook for 40 minutes, stirring occasionally.

Meanwhile, make the fried leeks. Remove the outer layer of the leek and discard it, then wash the leek and halve it lengthways. Cut each half into thirds, then thinly slice the thirds into thin strips. Add the remaining vegetable oil to a cold frying pan along with the sliced leeks. Make sure the leeks cover the entire surface area of the pan. Turn the heat to medium and then slowly fry the leeks without moving them for 8–10 minutes. Once they start turning dark golden brown, stir occasionally until the majority of the leeks have turned the same colour. Remove the leeks from the oil, place on a plate and sprinkle with a pinch of salt.

Place the same pan back over a high heat and fry the eggs for 1–2 minutes until the edges are brown and crispy but the yolks are still runny. Set aside.

After 40 minutes, the liquid in the braised beef should have reduced but still be quite runny. Add the frozen peas and then slowly pour in the cornflour slurry while stirring. The sauce should thicken, but not be too thick. If the sauce is too thick, add splashes of cold water and stir to loosen it up.

Grab some bowls and put a generous amount of rice into each one. Generously ladle on the minced beef until the rice is covered completely. Sprinkle over the sesame seeds and coriander and drizzle on some chilli oil. Add a fried egg and some crispy leeks and enjoy.

HONEY-ROASTED CUMIN CHICKEN WITH SESAME RICE

PREP TIME 20 MINUTES
SERVES 2-4
COOK TIME 50 MINUTES

Here we have sweet and earthy cumin-roasted spatchcocked chicken, served with sesame rice cooked in rich chicken stock and a ribbon salad that uses a great vegetable peeler hack. The trick is to utilise the pan juice, as that's where the flavour is – deglaze and scrape up all of those golden caramelised chicken bits! Spatchcocking the chicken cuts the cooking time and provides crispier skin and juicier meat.

1 tbsp ground cumin
1 tbsp Chinese five-spice powder
2 tbsp garlic powder
2 tbsp light brown soft sugar
1 tbsp Sichuan peppercorns (optional)
3 tbsp vegetable oil
1.5kg chicken
400g jasmine rice
1 tbsp sesame oil
1 thumb-sized piece of fresh ginger, very finely chopped
1 tbsp sesame seeds
750ml chicken stock
1 tbsp unsalted butter
1 tbsp honey
2 tbsp light soy sauce
salt and freshly ground black pepper

For the salad
1 carrot, peeled lengthways with a vegetable peeler
1 cucumber, peeled lengthways with a vegetable peeler
½ red onion, thinly sliced
small bunch of coriander, roughly chopped
small bunch of mint, roughly chopped

For the salad dressing
1 tbsp honey
1 tbsp Chinese black vinegar (or balsamic vinegar)
1 tbsp light soy sauce

Preheat the oven to 200°C/180°C fan/gas mark 6.

Put the cumin, five-spice powder, garlic powder, sugar, Sichuan peppercorns (if using), a large pinch of salt, a few cracks of black pepper and the vegetable oil into a bowl. Stir thoroughly to create a paste.

Face the chicken breast side down, spine facing up on a board. Use a strong pair of scissors to cut along each side of the spine. Discard the spine and flip the chicken over. With the palm of your hands, press down with some force to flatten the chicken – you should hear a crack. Rub the marinade paste on both sides of the chicken, making sure to completely cover all the chicken. Place the chicken skin side up on a baking tray and roast in the oven for 40 minutes.

Meanwhile, put the rice into a bowl and cover with cold water. Rinse the rice and then pour out the water. Repeat this twice, or until the water is clear, then drain.

Heat the sesame oil in a saucepan over a medium heat and add two thirds of the ginger. Fry for 2–3 minutes, then add the sesame seeds and drained rice, followed by 625ml of the chicken stock and a large pinch of salt. Stir once, then cover, increase the heat to high and bring to the boil. Once boiling, reduce the heat to the lowest setting. Cook for 18 minutes without lifting the lid, then remove from the heat and set aside.

FEEDING A CROWD? DISHES TO SHARE

Combine all the ingredients for the salad in a bowl and toss together.

Combine all the ingredients for the dressing in a small bowl and set aside.

Remove the chicken from the oven and transfer it to a chopping board to rest for 15 minutes.

Meanwhile, place the baking tray with the chicken drippings over a medium heat. Fry the remaining ginger for 30 seconds, then add the remaining chicken stock to deglaze, using a wooden spoon to scrape up the burnt and golden edges to dissolve into the stock. Add the butter, honey, soy sauce and a pinch of salt. Cook for 1 minute, stirring well. Transfer to a bowl and set aside.

Once rested, slice the chicken down the middle between both breasts to cut in half.

Put a generous portion of rice on each plate, followed by half the chicken. Add the salad dressing to the salad and toss to coat. Add a handful of salad alongside the chicken. Generously spoon the pan sauce over the chicken. Enjoy.

(See photo overleaf)

KIMCHI PORK BELLY

PREP TIME 20 MINUTES
SERVES 4-6
COOK TIME 2½ HOURS

Who could say no to tender, fatty, spicy pork? Braised with loads of onions and kimchi, the fat renders into the sauce to make a mouthful of heaven – it well and truly bangs! Eat with lettuce wraps loaded up with rice, cucumber pickle, tangy soy onions and spring onion salad – this is real party food.

2 tbsp vegetable oil
1kg pork belly, cut into 6cm chunks
pinch of salt
1 large onion, sliced
300g kimchi, roughly chopped
500ml chicken stock
2 iceberg lettuces
cooked Japanese short-grain rice (see page 23), to serve

For the paste
5 garlic cloves, roughly chopped
2 tsp light brown soft sugar
1 tbsp gochujang paste
1 tbsp gochugaru (Korean red pepper flakes; or equal quantities paprika, cayenne pepper and chilli flakes)
1 tbsp sesame oil
5 tbsp light soy sauce
1 tbsp fish sauce
pinch of freshly ground black pepper

For the cucumber pickle
1 cucumber, thinly sliced
1 tbsp light soy sauce
3 tbsp rice vinegar
1 tsp granulated sugar
1 tsp sesame oil
1 tsp salt
1 tsp chilli oil

For the soy onions
1 onion, thinly sliced
juice of 1 lemon
1 tbsp light soy sauce

For the spring onion salad
3 spring onions, sliced into strips
1 garlic clove, finely chopped
1 tbsp light soy sauce
1 tbsp rice vinegar
1 tsp granulated sugar
1 tsp sesame seeds
1 tsp sesame oil
1 tsp gochugaru (see above)

Mix together the ingredients for the paste in a small bowl until thoroughly combined, then set aside.

Heat the vegetable oil in a heavy-based casserole dish over a medium-high heat for 2–3 minutes, then add the pork belly and salt. Sear the pork belly pieces for 3 minutes on each side until nicely golden. Add the onion and stir-fry for 1–2 minutes, then add the kimchi, juice and all, and fry for a further 2 minutes. Add the paste, followed by the chicken stock, and stir to combine. Bring to the boil, then cover and reduce to the lowest heat. Cook for 2 hours, checking every 30 minutes to make sure it is not catching on the bottom. If it is, add 100ml water and gently stir once or twice to loosen anything on the bottom.

After 2 hours, remove the lid and increase the heat to high. Cook for 3–5 minutes, stirring regularly, until the sauce has thickened but is not burnt and dry. Remove from the heat and leave to rest for 5–10 minutes. Meanwhile, make the side dishes.

For the cucumber pickle, combine the cucumber and salt in a bowl, mix to coat well and set aside for 3–5 minutes. The salt will draw the excess moisture from the cucumber. Squeeze the cucumber over the sink to drain the excess liquid, pour out the liquid from the bowl and then place the cucumber back into the bowl. Add the remaining ingredients and mix until thoroughly combined.

For the soy onions, combine all the ingredients in a bowl and toss until coated.

For the spring onion salad, put the spring onions into a bowl of cold water, leave to sit for 2–3 minutes and then drain. Add back to the bowl along with the other ingredients and mix until thoroughly coated.

When you're ready to serve, place all the bowls on the table along with the pork belly, rice and lettuce leaves. Use your fork to break off a piece of the pork belly and place in a lettuce leaf along with some braised kimchi, a spoonful of rice, some cucumber, onion and spring onion salad. Wrap up and enjoy!

CUMIN AND POTATO BRAISED LEG OF LAMB

PREP TIME 10 MINUTES
SERVES 4-6
COOK TIME 2½ HOURS

An easy one-pot wonder, this leg of lamb with Chinese flavours is slow-cooked until it's fall-off-the-bone tender. Traditionally, these types of 'braised' dishes are eaten with a bowl of steaming white rice but have it however you'd like. I have found this dish to be so versatile – you can even use it as a sandwich filling!

3 tbsp vegetable oil
2kg leg of lamb
10 garlic cloves, peeled
1 large thumb-sized piece of fresh ginger, thinly sliced
3 star anise
1 cinnamon stick
2 tbsp cumin seeds, toasted and crushed
4 dried whole chillies or 1–2 tbsp chilli flakes
1.5 litres chicken stock
10 round shallots, peeled
4 spring onions, cut into thirds
150ml light soy sauce
150ml dark soy sauce
2 tbsp oyster sauce
4 tbsp hoisin sauce
3 tbsp smooth peanut butter
50g rock sugar or 3 tbsp light brown soft sugar
4 large potatoes, peeled and quartered
2 carrots, cut into chunks
250g water chestnuts (optional)

To serve
large bunch of coriander, roughly chopped
2 spring onions, thinly sliced
1 tbsp sesame seeds, toasted
1 tbsp sesame oil

Preheat the oven to 190°C/170°C fan/gas mark 5.

Heat a large, deep heavy-based casserole dish (one that will fit the leg of lamb in with the lid on – I use a 6.3 litre Le Creuset) over a high heat. Add the vegetable oil and then sear the lamb for 2–3 minutes on all sides until golden brown all over. Remove the lamb and add the garlic, ginger, star anise, cinnamon stick cumin seeds and chillies. Fry for 1 minute until fragrant, then place the leg of lamb back in. Add the chicken stock followed by the shallots and spring onions. Finally, add the light and dark soy sauce, oyster sauce, hoisin sauce, peanut butter and sugar. Give it a stir to make sure everything has dissolved into the stock, then cover and bring to the boil. Once boiling, transfer to the oven and cook for 1½ hours.

After 1½ hours, add the potatoes, carrots and water chestnuts, making sure they're submerged. Cover again and return to the oven, then cook for a further 45 minutes.

Remove the dish from the oven and allow it to rest for 20 minutes without removing the lid. Once rested, use two forks to shred the meat into large chunks and remove the bone. Using a spoon, discard the layer of fat on top.

Garnish the braised lamb with the coriander, spring onions, sesame seeds and a drizzle of sesame oil.

FEEDING A CROWD? DISHES TO SHARE

FEELING HUNGOVER?

SIMPLE & COMFORTING

For me, the hangover usually be hanging . . . if it doesn't for you, I'm envious. The struggle of getting out of bed is real, and it's difficult to stop the intrusive thoughts of opening your phone and ordering food after an already expensive night. Hungover or not, these recipes will hit the spot and help you recover from whatever happened the night before – expect a lot of spice to reawaken those taste buds.

SPICY MISO BEEF UDON SOUP

PREP TIME 5 MINUTES
SERVES 1
COOK TIME 10 MINUTES

A bowl of nourishing noodles should be in everyone's repertoire, no exceptions. This is one of the easiest one-pot noodle soups you'll ever learn to cook – it really is so simple. You might have guessed that udon are one of my favourite noodles, and there's a reason for that. They're chewy, they don't overcook and, most importantly, they don't taint the broth, making them perfect for one-pot noodle soups!

2 tsp sesame oil
1 garlic clove, very finely chopped
100g thinly sliced beef from an Asian supermarket (or very thinly sliced rib-eye steak)
¼ onion, thinly sliced
20g shiitake mushrooms, thinly sliced
50g daikon (optional), thinly sliced
1 tsp chilli powder
500ml beef stock
pinch of salt
5g dried wakame seaweed (optional)
1 tsp gochujang paste (or chilli oil mixed with 1 tsp granulated sugar)
250g packet of frozen (or fresh) udon noodles
1 pak choi, trimmed and leaves separated
2 tsp white miso paste
1 spring onion, thinly sliced

Put the sesame oil and garlic into a saucepan over a high heat and fry for 1 minute, or until fragrant. Add the beef, onion, mushrooms, radish and chilli powder and fry for a further 2 minutes. Pour in the beef stock, then add the salt, wakame and gochujang, cover and boil for 3 minutes. Next, add the noodles and pak choi and cook for a further 3 minutes.

Put the miso paste and 1 tablespoon of the broth into a bowl and stir until combined into a runny paste. Remove the soup from the heat and pour in the miso mixture. Stir to combine. Serve the soup in a deep bowl, garnished with the spring onion.

CHICKEN TERIYAKI BRIOCHE BURGER

PREP TIME 10 MINUTES
SERVES 2
COOK TIME 20 MINUTES

This is a homage to a burger I accidentally discovered in Japan while searching for food in a state of hunger. It was comprised of the fluffiest, sweetest toasted brioche bun with a buttery aroma, and sandwiched in between, a juicy chicken teriyaki thigh fillet with a large dollop of Japanese mayo and crunchy lettuce. I still dream of it, but you don't have to, because here's the recipe!

1 tbsp unsalted butter
2 brioche burger buns, sliced in half
2 skin-on boneless chicken thighs
1 tbsp rice vinegar
2 tbsp light soy sauce
2 tbsp mirin
2 tbsp cooking sake (optional)
2 tbsp light brown soft sugar
1 garlic clove, grated
2cm piece of fresh ginger, grated
1 tsp cornflour mixed with 2 tbsp cold water
½ red onion, diced
2 slices of American cheese
2 leaves of iceberg lettuce, thinly sliced
Japanese mayonnaise (preferably Kewpie)
large bunch of chives, thinly sliced
salt and freshly ground black pepper

Melt the butter in a frying pan over a medium heat, then add the buns cut side down and toast for 2–3 minutes until golden, checking occasionally so they don't burn. Remove from the pan and set aside.

Season the chicken thighs with salt and pepper on both sides. Lay them skin side down in a cold pan and turn the heat to high. Cook for 5 minutes without moving them, then flip and cook for a further 5 minutes. Remove from the pan and set aside.

Lower the heat to medium-low. Add the vinegar, light soy sauce, mirin, sake (if using) and sugar. Add the garlic and ginger and swirl the pan for 1–2 minutes until the sugar has dissolved. Slowly pour in the cornflour and water slurry while stirring. The sauce should thicken and be glossy but not too thick. If it's too thick, add a splash of water. Remove the pan from the heat and add the chicken, flipping it to glaze both sides.

Put the red onion into a bowl of cold water to remove the harshness.

Put a slice of cheese onto the bottom of the buns, followed by a piece of chicken, some red onion, lettuce, a generous dollop of mayo and chives. Finally, top with the other half of the brioche bun.

FISH SAUCE CHICKEN WINGS

These Thai-inspired crispy fried wings marinated in fish sauce have a sort of surf-and-turf flavour situation going on. I serve them dunked into a spicy, tangy dipping sauce that is thickened with toasted rice powder for extra depth of flavour! Crack open a beer and you're living.

1kg chicken wings
4 tbsp plain flour
4 tbsp cornflour
¼ tsp bicarbonate of soda
½ tsp ground white pepper
120ml fish sauce
1 tsp MSG
½ tsp salt
3 tsp jasmine rice
juice of 4 limes
3 tbsp light brown soft sugar
3 tsp chilli flakes
small bunch of coriander, thinly sliced
1 spring onion, finely chopped
600ml vegetable oil
1 banana shallot, thinly sliced
small bunch of mint, thinly sliced

Put the chicken wings into a large bowl along with the flour, cornflour, bicarbonate of soda, white pepper, half the fish sauce, the MSG and salt. Mix well until fully coated. Set aside while you make the sauce.

Put the rice into a dry frying pan over a medium heat and toast for 3–4 minutes, shaking the pan regularly. Once golden brown, transfer to a pestle and mortar and pound until ground but not too fine. Alternatively, use a spice grinder or small food processor.

Next, combine the lime juice, the remaining fish sauce, brown sugar, chilli flakes, rice powder, coriander and spring onion in a bowl. Stir until the sugar has dissolved.

Heat the oil in a large saucepan over a medium-high heat until it reaches 175°C. To test the oil, hold a chopstick in the pan. If bubbles rapidly form around the chopstick, the oil is ready. Gently drop the wings into the oil one by one. Cook for 5–7 minutes, or until dark golden brown, flipping occasionally. Remove the wings and let them rest for a few minutes.

Place the wings on a platter and sprinkle over the sliced shallot and mint leaves. Serve with the sauce on the side.

STEAK SANDO

Japanese but with a Western twist, this is a top tier sando – its middle name is decadent. There's so much sauce it might as well have been called 'honey garlic sauce with a side of sando'! Japanese bread often has added sugar and is therefore sweeter, so I've gone for brioche. The high butter content also means it toasts perfectly, almost like toast out of a picture book or cartoon. Choose a steak that's tender, like fillet or rib-eye. The key is to slice the steak as thinly as possible.

4 garlic cloves, very finely chopped
5 tbsp light soy sauce
1 tbsp apple cider vinegar
1 tbsp light brown soft sugar
1 tbsp clear honey
100ml water
1 tbsp cornflour mixed with 50ml water, or as needed
1 tbsp unsalted butter
4 slices of brioche
4 slices of American cheese
1 tbsp olive oil
250g rib-eye steak (or another steak of your choice)
pinch of salt
1 tomato, sliced
handful of rocket

Combine the garlic, soy sauce, vinegar, sugar, honey and water in a small saucepan over a medium heat and simmer for 3 minutes, then remove from the heat. Slowly pour in the cornflour and water slurry while stirring. The sauce should be smooth with the consistency of gravy. If it's too thin, add a bit more, if it's too thick add a splash of water.

Heat the butter in a frying pan over a medium heat and gently toast the brioche for about 1 minute on each side. Keep an eye on it so it doesn't burn. Remove from the pan and place a slice of cheese on each slice of brioche.

Using the same pan, increase the heat to high and then add the oil. Season the steaks with the salt, then place in the pan and cook for 2 minutes on each side for medium-rare. Remove from the pan and set aside to rest on a plate for 5 minutes.

Once rested, slice the steak into thin strips, removing any bits of fat. Stack the steak on two of the slices of bread and generously coat with the sauce. Top with the sliced tomato, followed by a handful of rocket. Press down with another slice of bread to complete the sandwiches. Cut in half and enjoy!

THINLY SLICED STEAK WITH CITRUS SAUCE

PREP TIME 10 MINUTES
SERVES 1
COOK TIME 5 MINUTES

Here's one of my favourite quick summer recipes, which also works as a show-stopping starter for dinner parties. Sirloin steak is cooked rare, thinly sliced and then served with a pool of citrusy sauce, garlic chips, coriander, red onion and chilli to tingle the taste buds. I've had many people asking to drink the sauce after the steak has all gone! To eat, grab a slice of steak, add coriander, red onion and chilli to the middle and roll it up, then dunk into the sauce and enjoy!

200–250g sirloin steak
2 garlic cloves, thinly sliced
2 tbsp olive oil
½ red onion, thinly sliced and placed in ice-cold water
small bunch of coriander, leaves picked
1 red chilli, thinly sliced
salt and freshly ground black pepper

For the citrus sauce
juice of 1 lime
juice of 1 lemon
3 tbsp light soy sauce
½ tsp granulated sugar
½ tsp MSG
1 tsp dashi powder (optional)

Season the steak with salt and black pepper on both sides. Set aside.

Put the garlic slices into a bowl of water and then drain and pat dry with kitchen paper. This step will stop the garlic from burning and tasting bitter. Transfer the garlic to a frying pan along with half the oil, then fry over a medium heat for 2–3 minutes, or until lightly golden brown. While frying, tilt the pan to the side to fully submerge the garlic chips. Transfer the garlic and oil to a small bowl and set aside.

Heat the remaining oil in the same pan over a high heat for 2 minutes. Cook the steak for 1 minute on each side for rare. Using a pair of tongs, hold the steak fat side down for 30 seconds, then remove from the pan and leave to rest for 3 minutes while you make the sauce.

To make the sauce, combine all the ingredients in a bowl and whisk.

Slice the steak as thinly as possible, then place it on a plate with high edges. Pour the sauce onto the plate around the steak. Spoon the garlic chips and oil onto the steak. Add the drained red onion on top in a line down the middle, followed by the coriander. Add the thinly sliced chilli to the side in a pile.

To serve, grab a slice of steak, place a coriander leaf, slice of red onion and slice of chilli in the middle and roll. Dunk in the sauce and enjoy.

SPICY PORK BAKED POTATO

A creation born out of accident and luck. I had leftover braised pork but no rice. Enter the holy potato. As a British-born Chinese person, I've grown up eating the classic jacket potato. While there was nothing wrong with it, it needed something punchier . . . something spicy? One hungover morning I woke up and, to my horror, realised I had no more rice (shock). Thirsting for some well-needed nutrients, I combined what was in the fridge . . . and the almighty Spicy Pork Baked Potato was born. Baked potatoes usually take an hour to cook in the oven, but with this microwave hack it only takes 25 minutes.

2 large potatoes
4 tbsp salted butter
olive oil, for rubbing
salt

For the spicy braised pork
glug of olive oil
1 white onion, diced
1 carrot, diced
4 garlic cloves, very finely chopped
1 thumb-sized piece of fresh ginger, grated
2 red chillies, chopped
1 star anise
200g minced pork
1 tbsp doubanjiang (fermented chilli bean paste) or gochujang paste
1 tbsp light soy sauce
1 tbsp oyster sauce
1 tsp granulated sugar
500ml chicken stock
1 tbsp sesame oil

To serve
1 tbsp sesame seeds
small bunch of coriander, thinly sliced
1 spring onion, thinly sliced
chilli oil (optional)

First, make the spicy braised pork. Heat a heavy-based saucepan over a high heat for around 1 minute, then add the oil. Add the onion, carrot, garlic, ginger, chilli and star anise and fry for 2 minutes, then add the minced pork and use a wooden spoon to break it up, ensuring there are no clumps of meat. Brown the mince for 5 minutes, or until the liquid has evaporated.

Next, add the doubanjiang and fry for 1 minute, then add the soy sauce, oyster sauce, sugar and chicken stock. Cover and bring to the boil, then reduce the heat to medium-low and cook for 20 minutes, stirring occasionally to make sure it isn't sticking to the bottom.

Preheat the oven to 200°C/180°C fan/gas mark 6.

Using a fork, poke holes all over the potatoes. Rub with olive oil and sprinkle lightly with salt. Place the potatoes on a microwavable plate and cover with a bowl. Microwave for 4 minutes on high, then flip the potato and microwave for a further 4 minutes. Put the potatoes into the oven and cook for 15 minutes.

Remove the pork from the heat and stir in the sesame oil.

Remove the potatoes from the oven and cut a cross in the tops to open them up.

Put 1 tablespoon of the butter into each potato and use a fork to mash the butter and potato until combined, then add a final tablespoon of butter on the top of the potatoes.

Put the potatoes on plates and generously spoon the sauce on top. Garnish with the sesame seeds, coriander and spring onion, then drizzle with your favourite chilli oil if you like.

FEELING HUNGOVER? SIMPLE & COMFORTING

SIZZLING BEEF PEPPER RICE WITH HONEY-GARLIC SAUCE

PREP TIME 10 MINUTES
SERVES 2
COOK TIME 17 MINUTES

If I could I'd eat this every day . . . actually, that is what I did in Japan! Served on a sizzling plate (or pan, in this case), this genuinely couldn't be easier to make. Essentially, it's white rice with a knob of butter, medium-rare steak, sweetcorn and spring onions, finished off with a small (big) drizzle of honey and garlic soy sauce. Pour it into the pan and let the whole thing steam and sizzle, then bring it to your table and eat it straight out of the pan – one of those kinda days!

300g rib-eye steak
1 tbsp light soy sauce
1 tsp freshly ground black pepper, plus extra for the rice
pinch of salt
1 tbsp vegetable oil
400g cooked Japanese short-grain rice (see page 23)
1 tbsp unsalted butter
1 x 200g tin of sweetcorn, drained
2 spring onions, thinly sliced
1 tsp cayenne pepper (optional)

For the honey-garlic sauce
2 tsp vegetable oil
½ onion, diced
3 garlic cloves, smashed
100ml light soy sauce
100ml clear honey
1 tbsp cornstarch mixed with 1 tbsp water

First, make the sauce. Heat the oil in a saucepan over a medium heat and gently fry the onion and garlic for 2–3 minutes until starting to soften. Add the soy sauce and honey and simmer for a further 1–2 minutes, then slowly pour in the cornflour slurry sauce until the sauce starts to thicken (you might not need all of the slurry). The consistency should be thick like a gravy. Once thick, simmer for a further 30 seconds or until it starts to slowly bubble. Transfer to a blender and allow to cool, then blend until smooth. Pour into a bowl and set aside.

Season the steak with the soy sauce, black pepper and salt.

Heat the vegetable oil in a frying pan over a high heat until almost smoking, then cook the steak for 1–2 minutes on each side for medium-rare. Remove the steak and leave to rest for 3–5 minutes, then slice it into 1–2cm slices.

Place the pan back over a high heat. Spoon the rice into a bowl and press it down to pack it in. Turn the bowl out onto the pan so you have a mound of rice. Place the butter on top and finish with a few cracks of black pepper. Add the sweetcorn alongside the rice, then place the steak into the pan, slightly fanned out. Sprinkle generously with the spring onions and cayenne pepper (if using). Finally, pour the sauce around the pan and watch it sizzle! Remove from the heat and transfer the pan to the table. Stir the rice to combine it with the sauce and sweetcorn before eating.

BAKED BLACK PEPPER PRAWN GLASS NOODLES

PREP TIME 10 MINUTES
SERVES 1
COOK TIME 10 MINUTES

Another one-pot classic noodle dish to grace your kitchen. This recipe is inspired by my travels in Bangkok – I genuinely couldn't get enough of these moreish seafood glass noodles, but the glue that brought it all together was the spicy lime sauce. These glass noodles soak up flavour like a sponge. If you have a claypot, use it! But it's definitely not necessary.

200ml water
2 tbsp dark soy sauce
1 tsp light soy sauce
2 tsp fish sauce
1 tsp oyster sauce
1 tsp granulated sugar
1 tsp freshly ground black pepper
50g glass noodles
1 spring onion
½ celery stick
2 tsp unsalted butter
50g fresh ginger, very finely chopped
3 garlic cloves, very finely chopped
1 tsp sesame oil
75g cooked peeled king prawns, butterflied
1 tsp sesame seeds

For the spicy lime sauce
1 red chilli
small bunch of coriander
juice of 1 lime
2 tsp fish sauce
1 tsp granulated sugar

Combine the water, dark and light soy sauce, 1 teaspoon of the fish sauce, oyster sauce, sugar and black pepper in a large bowl and stir until the sugar has dissolved. Submerge the glass noodles in the liquid and set aside.

Cut the spring onion into thirds, then slice the thirds lengthways as thinly as possible, into strips. Do the same for the celery.

Next, make the spicy lime sauce. Combine all the ingredients in a small food processor and blend until fine. Pour into a small bowl and set aside.

Put the butter, ginger and garlic into a frying pan over a medium-high heat and cook for 2–3 minutes, or until the garlic has turned golden. Remove from the heat and add the remaining 1 teaspoon of fish sauce. Stir to combine, then set aside.

Pour the sesame oil into a saucepan or claypot over a high heat, then add the noodles and their soaking liquid. Cover and bring to the boil, then lower the heat to medium and cook for a further 5 minutes, or until the liquid has mostly evaporated. Stir the noodles occasionally so they don't stick to the bottom. Once the liquid has evaporated, remove the pan from the heat and add the prawns around the side of the pot. Pour the garlic butter over the noodles and prawns. Top with the sliced spring onion and celery. Put the lid back on and leave to sit for 3 minutes. Drizzle over the spicy lime sauce just before eating, then give it a mix and enjoy.

CRISPY CHICKEN KATSU SANDO

Something about fried chicken sandwiches just calls to me all day, every day. I mean, have you ever had one that didn't bang? In Japan, they eat katsu with a bowl of white rice, tonkatsu sauce (think fruity and tangy) and the thinnest shredded cabbage you'll ever see! This is my version of the classic chicken katsu sando (the Japanese word for sandwich), which incorporates all the best elements between two slices of soft white bread.

4 large slices of thick white bread, crusts cut off
4 tbsp unsalted butter, softened
2 chicken breasts
100g plain flour
2 medium eggs, beaten
150g panko breadcrumbs
250ml vegetable oil, or as needed
4 slices of American cheese
3–4 tbsp Japanese mayonnaise, such as Kewpie
½ white cabbage, thinly shredded
small bunch of coriander, roughly chopped
small bunch of chives, finely chopped
salt

For the cucumber pickles
½ cucumber, thinly sliced
1 tsp salt
1 tbsp light soy sauce
1 tbsp rice vinegar
1 tsp sesame oil
1 tsp sesame seeds

For the sauce
100ml tomato ketchup
40ml oyster sauce
75ml Worcestershire sauce
30g granulated sugar
few drops of Tabasco (optional)
1 tsp sesame seeds

First, make the cucumber pickles. Combine the cucumber and salt in a bowl, mix to coat well and set aside for 5 minutes. The salt will draw the excess moisture from the cucumber. Squeeze the cucumber over the sink to drain the excess liquid, pour out the liquid from the bowl and then place the cucumber back into the bowl. Add the remaining ingredients and mix well to combine. Set aside.

Next, make the sauce. Combine all the ingredients in a bowl and stir until the sugar has dissolved. Set aside.

Spread the bread with the butter on both sides. Heat a large frying pan over a medium heat and toast the bread for 1–2 minutes on each side until golden, then remove from the pan and set aside.

Place a chicken breast on one side of a piece of baking paper, fold the rest of the paper over the top and bash the chicken with a rolling pin until it is 2.5cm thick. Repeat with the remaining breast, then season with a pinch of salt on both sides.

Put the flour into a shallow dish, the beaten eggs into a separate dish, and the breadcrumbs into a third dish. Season the flour and the breadcrumbs with a generous pinch of salt and stir to combine.

Pour the oil into the frying pan you toasted the bread in – it should be about 2.5cm deep – and set over a medium heat.

While the oil is heating, dip a chicken breast into the flour, making sure to cover every part. Lift up and gently dust off any excess flour, then add it to the eggs and coat thoroughly. Lastly, add the chicken to the breadcrumbs and cover thoroughly. Use your hands to push and pack the breadcrumbs onto the chicken. Repeat with the remaining breast.

Gently place the chicken into the pan and cook for 2–3 minutes, then flip and cook for a further 2–3 minutes, basting the top of the chicken with oil from the pan using a spoon. Once golden brown, remove from the pan and place on a plate. Place two slices of cheese on top to melt.

Spread the mayonnaise over two slices of the bread, then place a chicken breast on the bread without mayo. Generously spoon the sauce over the chicken, then add a large handful of cabbage, followed by the coriander and chives and finally the cucumber pickles. Close the sandwiches with the other slice of bread and cut in half. Enjoy!

(See photo overleaf)

VOLCANO CHILLI CHICKEN

PREP TIME 15 MINUTES
SERVES 2
COOK TIME 25 MINUTES

It's in the name – this dish is not for the faint hearted! Chilli, chicken, sweetcorn are combined with melted mozzarella for the most insane cheese pulls. It's a deadly but heavenly combo, and definitely one for a night of beer! Serve this sharing dish with bowls of steaming rice – you'll need it as a fire blanket for your mouth!

1 tbsp vegetable oil
6 skinless and boneless chicken thighs, cut into 2–3cm pieces
1 green chilli, thinly sliced
½ x 200g tin of sweetcorn, drained
150g pre-shredded mozzarella
1 spring onion, thinly sliced
1 sheet of nori seaweed, cut into thin strips (optional)
cooked Japanese short-grain rice (see page 23), to serve

For the sauce
1 tbsp gochujang paste
4 tbsp gochugaru (Korean red pepper flakes)
1 tbsp light brown soft sugar
1 tbsp clear honey
1 tbsp chicken stock powder or 1 chicken stock cube, crumbled
1 tbsp light soy sauce
1 tbsp oyster sauce
3 tbsp mirin
½ tbsp freshly ground black pepper
1 tsp sesame oil
3 garlic cloves, finely chopped
1cm piece of fresh ginger, finely chopped
25ml water

First, combine all the ingredients for the sauce in a bowl and set aside.

Heat the vegetable oil in a frying pan or wok over a high heat for about 1 minute, then add the chicken and stir-fry for 3–4 minutes, or until nicely golden brown. Lower the heat to medium and pour in the sauce, then add the sliced chilli. Toss to coat and stir-fry for a further 2–3 minutes, or until the sauce has thoroughly coated and stuck to the chicken. Transfer to a small ovenproof plate or dish and sprinkle with the sweetcorn and then the mozzarella.

Preheat the grill on high. Make sure the oven shelf below the grill is as high as possible. Place the dish in the oven and cook for 3–4 minutes, or until the cheese has melted and browned in places. Remove from the oven and sprinkle with the sliced spring onion and shredded nori. Place the dish on the table and enjoy with a bowl of steaming rice (and beer, if you like).

FUJIAN FRIED RICE WITH CHICKEN, PRAWN AND CHINESE SAUSAGE

PREP TIME 15 MINUTES
SERVES 2–4
COOK TIME 20 MINUTES

Egg fried rice, slathered with a rich, thick umami gravy filled with vegetables, prawns, chicken and Chinese sausage. One of my favourite dishes to order in a Chinese restaurant growing up and still to this day – it's not a side dish, it's the MAIN dish! I could genuinely eat a portion for two, so the more the better for this one!

For the gravy
500ml chicken stock
1 tbsp oyster sauce
1 tbsp light soy sauce
1 tbsp dark soy sauce
1 tsp sesame oil
1 tsp granulated sugar
¼ tsp ground white pepper
1–2 tbsp cornflour mixed with 1–2 tbsp water

For the fried rice
2 tbsp vegetable oil
2 large eggs, beaten
400g cooked jasmine rice (see page 23)
½ tsp granulated sugar
½ tsp salt
1 tbsp light soy sauce
1 spring onion, thinly sliced
1 tbsp water

For the topping
1 tbsp vegetable oil
1 Chinese sausage, diced
1 skinless and boneless chicken thigh, cut into 1cm pieces
5 raw shelled king prawns, cut into 1cm pieces
5 dried or fresh shiitake mushrooms (soaked if dried), diced
50g carrot, finely diced
¼ banana shallot, finely chopped
2 garlic cloves, finely chopped
75g frozen peas
salt

First, combine all the ingredients for the gravy except the cornflour slurry in a bowl and stir until the sugar has dissolved. Set aside.

Next, make the fried rice. Heat the oil in a wok or large frying pan over a high heat for 2–3 minutes until smoking, then add the eggs and scramble vigorously for 30–45 seconds. Add the rice and toss to incorporate the egg. Add the sugar, salt and soy sauce, followed by the spring onion and water. Stir-fry for a further 1–2 minutes, stirring continuously so it doesn't catch or burn on the bottom. Divide the rice between shallow bowls and set aside while you make the gravy.

Give the pan a wipe with kitchen paper to remove any burnt bits, then place it back over a medium-high heat. Add the oil, Chinese sausage, chicken, prawns, mushrooms and carrot and stir-fry for 2–3 minutes until the ingredients are nicely seared but the chicken is not fully cooked. Add the shallot and garlic, followed by a pinch of salt. Stir-fry for a further 1 minute, then pour in the gravy and then the peas. Bring to a simmer. Once simmering, gently pour in the cornflour slurry while stirring. Bring the sauce back to a simmer and cook for 2–3 minutes until thickened. It should be thick and glossy – if it's too thin, add more slurry. Generously spoon the gravy over the fried rice and enjoy.

CHICKEN AND SWEETCORN RICE

PREP TIME 10 MINUTES
SERVES 2
COOK TIME 10 MINUTES

This is one of my guilty pleasures when I'm hungover and really just can't be bothered to cook. The inspiration actually comes from my childhood. I was a fussy child who wasn't that interested in food, so my mum would order me a chicken and sweetcorn soup and a bowl of rice and mix the two together so she wouldn't have to worry about me not eating.

1 x 200g tin of sweetcorn, drained (or if you can find creamed sweetcorn, even better!)
1 tbsp vegetable oil
2 skinless and boneless chicken thighs, finely chopped
250ml chicken stock
1 tbsp cornflour mixed with 1 tbsp water
1 medium egg, beaten with a pinch of salt
½ tsp sesame oil
½ spring onion, thinly sliced
300g cooked jasmine rice (see page 23)

For the seasoning

½ tsp chicken stock powder (or ½ chicken stock cube)
½ tsp salt
¼ tsp granulated sugar
¼ tsp MSG
½ tsp ground white pepper
1 tsp light soy sauce

Put the sweetcorn into a freezer or sandwich bag, seal and smash the corn with a rolling pin. The consistency should be slightly chunky. Skip this step if you're using creamed corn.

Heat the oil in a frying pan over a medium-high heat for 1 minute, then add the chicken and stir-fry for 1–2 minutes. Add the sweetcorn, chicken stock and all the seasonings. Bring to the boil, then reduce the heat to medium and simmer for 3–5 minutes until it has reduced by a quarter. Slowly pour in the cornflour slurry while stirring, then simmer for a further 1–2 minutes until thickened. Slowly pour the egg into the sauce and stir slowly with chopsticks. Simmer for a further 30–45 seconds, then remove from the heat.

To serve, stir in the sesame oil and spring onion, then ladle over the white rice in bowls.

SAUCY BRAISED CHICKEN NOODLES WITH SPICY BEANSPROUT SALAD

I crave saucy noodles almost daily and this is a super-simple, failsafe recipe that cooks the chicken until tender and shreddable and makes a rich and caramelised sauce from the braising liquid at the same time. I've paired this with a crunchy and tangy carrot and beansprout salad to give it some texture.

2 chicken legs
5 tbsp dark soy sauce
40g rock sugar
850ml water
2 spring onions
5 garlic cloves, peeled but left whole
1 thumb-sized piece of fresh ginger, lightly smashed
1 tsp MSG (optional)
1 cinnamon stick
1 star anise
4½ tbsp light soy sauce
pinch of salt
2 tbsp cornflour mixed with 2 tbsp cold water
2 packets of instant noodles (any type)
1 tbsp sesame oil

For the salad
½ carrot, cut into matchsticks
handful of beansprouts
1 spring onion, sliced
1 tsp light soy sauce
1 tsp rice vinegar
1 tsp chilli oil

Put the chicken into a bowl with 3 tablespoons of the dark soy sauce and massage until coated well.

Put the rock sugar and 3 tablespoons of the water into a saucepan over a medium heat and slowly stir to dissolve. Keep stirring until the water has evaporated and then until the sugar has caramelised to a deep brown colour – this should take 5–7 minutes. As soon as it has, pour in the remaining water.

Add the spring onion, the garlic cloves, ginger, MSG, cinnamon stick, star anise, the remaining dark soy sauce, 4 tablespoons of the light soy sauce and a generous pinch of salt. Cover and bring to the boil, then gently drop in the chicken along with any sauce from the bowl. Cover again, lower the heat to medium and cook for 15 minutes. After 15 minutes, remove from the heat and leave to sit for 30 minutes before transferring the chicken to a plate and allowing to cool. Keep the saucepan of sauce. Once the chicken has cooled, use a fork to shred the meat off the bone.

Meanwhile, make the salad. Bring a saucepan of water to the boil and cook the carrot and beansprouts for 30 seconds, then remove and place in a bowl. Keep the saucepan of water for later use. Add the sliced spring onion, soy sauce, rice vinegar and chilli oil to the vegetables and toss to combine.

Remove the aromatics from the sauce and increase the heat to high. Once boiling, remove from the heat and slowly pour in the cornflour slurry while stirring to thicken the sauce.

Bring the pan used for the beansprouts back to a boil and cook the noodles according to the packet instructions. Drain the noodles, then add back to the pan along with the sesame oil and remaining ½ tablespoon light soy sauce. Mix well to coat.

Plate the noodles, then add the shredded chicken on top and generously pour over the thickened sauce. Add a handful of the salad on the side to serve.

FEELING HUNGOVER? SIMPLE & COMFORTING

CHOPPED ROAST PORK GRAVY RICE

PLUS MARINATING TIME

Roasted meat on rice is arguably the most iconic and popular dish in all of Cantonese cuisine. And, correct me if I'm wrong, but the sauce is the best bit. Unpopular opinion? Perhaps. Cantonese roasted meats are cooked over fire or in wood-fired ovens, but here is my much easier and quicker oven method, which is sure to become a weekly staple!

300g pork belly strips
2 tbsp vegetable oil
2 large eggs
pinch of salt

For the marinade
2 tbsp light soy sauce
2 tbsp hoisin sauce
2 tsp Chinese five-spice powder
2 tsp clear honey
1 tsp light brown soft sugar
½ tsp ground white pepper
1 tbsp vegetable oil
1 tsp fermented red tofu (optional)
1 tsp Shaoxing wine (optional)

For the spring onion oil
3 spring onions, thinly sliced
3 tbsp vegetable oil
½ tsp salt
½ tsp granulated sugar
½ tsp MSG

For the gravy
150ml chicken stock
1 tbsp light soy sauce
1 tbsp dark soy sauce
1 tbsp oyster sauce
¼ tsp salt
1 tsp granulated sugar
pinch of MSG (optional)
1 tbsp cornflour mixed with 1 tbsp water

To serve
cooked jasmine rice (see page 23)
blanched pak choi

Using a fork, poke holes all over the pork belly – the more the better. Put the pork into a bowl and add the marinade ingredients, then mix well to coat thoroughly. Cover with cling film and set aside in the fridge to marinate for at least 30 minutes, or overnight if possible (the longer the better – you can leave this for 24 hours if you like).

Preheat the oven to 190°C/170°C fan/gas mark 5.

Transfer the pork belly to a baking tray lined with foil, reserving any leftover marinade. Roast the pork on the middle shelf of the oven for 30 minutes, flipping halfway through.

Meanwhile, make the spring onion oil and gravy.

Put the spring onions and oil into a frying pan over a medium-high heat and cook for 3–5 minutes, stirring regularly, until the spring onions start to turn slightly golden. Add the salt, sugar and MSG, stir to combine and then pour into a bowl.

(Recipe continues overleaf)

Combine all the ingredients for the gravy except the cornflour slurry in a saucepan and bring to the boil, then reduce the heat and simmer for 3–5 minutes until reduced by a quarter. Slowly pour the cornflour slurry into the pan while stirring, then simmer for a further 1–2 minutes until thick and glossy. If it's too thin, add more slurry.

After 30 minutes, remove the pork from the oven and brush it with the leftover marinade, then return to the oven to cook for a further 15 minutes, basting it every 5 minutes. The pork belly should be nicely charred on the edges. Remove from the oven and leave to rest for 5 minutes.

Next, make the crispy fried eggs. Heat the oil in a frying pan over a high heat for 1–2 minutes, then crack in the eggs and fry for 1–2 minutes, or until the edges are crispy and golden. Using a spoon, baste the top of the egg with hot oil to ensure the whites are cooked. Sprinkle with salt and remove from the pan.

Once the pork has rested, cut it into slices around 1cm thick. Divide the rice between plates and top with the pork, followed by an egg and blanched pak choi. Generously pour the gravy on top and finish with a few spoonfuls of the spring onion oil.

WANT TO TREAT YO' SELF? *SOMETHING SPECIAL*

After a long day, I find it important to relax and enjoy myself. I want to have some me and my food time – after all, food shouldn't be a chore. For many, it's what we look forward to all day. Have you met a single person that food can't cheer up? Sometimes we need to treat ourselves and these recipes do exactly that. From bougie to impressive, these will put a smile on your face after the longest of days.

STICKY GINGER AND GARLIC RIBS

These ribs are poached until super tender, then basted with a spicy, sticky, honey glaze and roasted until charred. With a sweet and tangy coriander dip to go with it, this is yet another beer snack to grace your kitchen!

1kg pork ribs, separated
1 onion, halved
1 tsp salt
3 garlic cloves

For the glaze
2 tbsp clear honey
2 tbsp light soy sauce
2 tbsp oyster sauce
2 tbsp dark soy sauce
1 tsp granulated sugar
1 tsp MSG (optional)
½ tsp ground white pepper
50ml water

For the dipping sauce
150ml rice vinegar
3 tbsp granulated sugar
1 tbsp light soy sauce
1 tbsp MSG
2cm piece of fresh ginger, very finely chopped
4 garlic cloves, very finely chopped
3 bird's eye chillies, very finely chopped
1 banana shallot, very finely chopped
small bunch of coriander, thinly sliced

Put the ribs, onion, salt and garlic into a large saucepan and fill with water. The ribs should be fully submerged. Cover and bring to the boil, then reduce the heat to low and cook for 45 minutes. Once cooked, drain the ribs and place on a baking tray to cool. Meanwhile make the glaze and dipping sauce.

For the glaze, combine all the ingredients in a bowl and set aside.

For the sauce, combine the vinegar, sugar, soy sauce and MSG in a bowl and stir until the sugar has fully dissolved. Add the remaining ingredients, stir well and set aside.

Preheat the oven to 220°C/200°C fan/gas mark 7.

Once the ribs have cooled, use a brush or spoon to glaze the ribs all over, then place on a rack over a baking tray or a tray lined with foil. Cook in the oven for 20 minutes, basting and flipping the ribs every 5 minutes, or until the ribs are dark, slightly charred and sticky.

Place the ribs on a large plate with the bowl of dipping sauce on the side and enjoy.

FIVE-SPICE SALT AND PEPPER SQUID BAGUETTE

Salt and pepper squid is a Chinese takeaway classic – one that I usually have to order more than one portion of because I have a few family members who are vultures and will eat the lot! Take the squid and stuff it into a baguette with lashings of spicy mayo and lettuce, and you have what I perceive as the love child of East meets West!

300g squid rings
1 medium egg yolk
½ tsp ground white pepper
½ tsp salt
1 tbsp potato starch (or cornflour)
500ml vegetable oil, or as needed
2 garlic cloves, finely chopped
½ onion, diced
½ red chilli, diced
½ green chilli, diced
1 spring onion, thinly sliced
2 small baguettes
½ iceberg lettuce, thinly shredded

For the batter
6 tbsp plain flour
3 tbsp potato starch (or cornflour)
6 tbsp cold water
1 tsp baking powder
½ tsp salt
1 tsp vegetable oil

For the spicy mayo
3 tbsp Japanese mayonnaise, such as Kewpie (or regular mayo)
zest and juice of 1 lime
1 tsp light soy sauce
1 tbsp sriracha
small bunch of chives, thinly sliced

For the five-spice salt
1 tsp Chinese five-spice powder
1 tsp salt
½ tsp granulated sugar
1 tsp MSG

Combine all the ingredients for the batter in a bowl and mix until smooth, then set aside.

Combine all the ingredients for the spicy mayo in a bowl, then set aside.

Combine all the ingredients for the five-spice salt in a small bowl, then set aside.

Put the squid rings into a bowl with the egg yolk, white pepper and salt. Mix well until the squid is fully coated, then add the potato starch and mix again until coated.

Heat at least 8cm oil in a large saucepan over a medium-high heat until it reaches 175°C. To test the oil, hold a chopstick in the pan. If bubbles rapidly form around the chopstick, the oil is ready.

Submerge the squid in the batter, ensuring it is thoroughly coated. Lower the squid rings into the oil one by one, then cook for 2–4 minutes, stirring occasionally to stop the squid from sticking, until it is golden and crispy. Remove from the oil with a slotted spoon and drain on kitchen paper.

Take 1 tablespoon of the oil you fried the squid in and heat it in a wok or large frying pan over a high heat for about 1 minute. Add the garlic, onion, chillies and spring onion and stir-fry for 1–2 minutes, or until slightly coloured. Add the squid to the pan and sprinkle with the five-spice salt. Toss for 30–45 seconds to evenly coat the squid.

Split open the baguettes and use your fingers to pull out some of the middle so that the filling will fit inside. Generously spread the spicy mayo on the bottom of the baguettes, then add the fried squid and top with lettuce.

CHEAT'S PRAWN AND CUCUMBER LAKSA

Laksa is one of my all-time favourite noodle soups. If you're not familiar, it's a curry-based noodle soup hailing from Southeast Asia. There are all sorts of variations – with egg noodles, rice noodles, coconut-based, seafood or chicken. This recipe is a cheat's version – something to give me a quick fix – so I apologise to any purists that may be reading this.

2 x 100g nests of rice vermicelli noodles (or egg noodles or instant noodles)
2 medium eggs
small bunch of mint, thinly sliced
small bunch of coriander, thinly sliced
1 tbsp vegetable oil
1 banana shallot, diced
2 tbsp laksa paste (or red curry paste)
400ml coconut milk
200ml chicken stock
1 tsp fish sauce, or as needed
½ tsp granulated sugar
100g cooked peeled king prawns
½ cucumber, cut into matchsticks
1 bird's eye chilli, thinly sliced
1 lime, cut into wedges
2 tsp hoisin sauce

Put the noodles into a bowl and cover with boiling water, then set aside to soak for 10 minutes. Once soaked, drain and divide between two ramen bowls.

Meanwhile, bring a saucepan of water to the boil and add the eggs. Cook for 5½ minutes, then drain and place in a bowl of cold water. Once cool, peel and slice in half. Set aside.

Mix the mint and coriander together and set aside.

Heat the oil in a saucepan over a medium-high heat, then add the shallot and fry for 1–2 minutes. Add the laksa paste and fry for a further minute, then add the coconut milk, chicken stock, fish sauce and sugar. Bring to the boil, then reduce the heat to medium and simmer for 5–7 minutes until reduced by a quarter. Taste the broth – it should be slightly over-salty. Adjust to your preference with more fish sauce.

Place the prawns on the noodles near the edge of the bowl. Ladle the soup into the bowls until the noodles are submerged, then place the eggs into the bowls, also near the edge. Heap a generous amount of coriander and mint in the middle of the bowl. Add the sliced cucumber next to the herbs. Sprinkle the red chilli over the top and garnish with the lime wedges. Put the hoisin sauce into soup spoons and rest them on top of the noodles. Mix the hoisin into the soup just before eating.

FRIED TOFU HO FUN v

PREP TIME 15 MINUTES
SERVES 2
COOK TIME 20 MINUTES

Most people think there are two categories for noodles, fried or soup, but there's actually a third, and it's insanely popular in East Asia. There's no specific name for it in English, but the Chinese name literally translates as 'mixed noodles'. Basically, it's fried noodles covered in a thick gravy – sounds banging, right? It lives in my head rent free even though, weirdly, it can be hard to find in the West.

400g ho fun noodles (or any noodles)
4–5 tbsp vegetable oil (or lard)
2 tsp dark soy sauce
½ tsp granulated sugar
2 garlic cloves, finely chopped
100g gai lan (Chinese broccoli) or Tenderstem broccoli, thinly sliced on the diagonal
250ml vegetable stock (or chicken stock)
1–2 tbsp cornstarch mixed with 1–2 tbsp water

For the chilli vinegar
1 red chilli, finely chopped
75ml distilled white vinegar or rice vinegar
½ tsp granulated sugar

For the tofu
250g extra-firm tofu, patted dry and cut into 2cm cubes
½ tbsp light soy sauce
½ tbsp vegetarian oyster sauce (or oyster sauce)
1½ tbsp cornflour
½ tsp salt
½ tsp ground white pepper

For the seasoning
½ tbsp dark soy sauce
2 tbsp light soy sauce (or fish sauce)
1 tsp granulated sugar
¼ tsp ground white pepper
¼ tsp MSG

To serve
1 tbsp chilli flakes
1 tbsp chilli oil

Bring a saucepan of water to the boil and cook the noodles for 1 minute less than the time stated on the packet, then drain and place on a plate to dry and cool for 10–15 minutes. If using fresh ho fun, pierce a few holes in the packet with a knife and microwave for 1–2 minutes.

Next, make the chilli vinegar. Combine all the ingredients in a bowl and stir until the sugar has dissolved, then set aside.

Now marinate the tofu. Put the tofu into a bowl and season with the soy sauce and oyster sauce. Mix well to coat evenly, then add the cornflour, salt and white pepper. Toss to coat.

Heat 2 tablespoons of the oil in a wok or large frying pan over a high heat for 1–2 minutes, then add the noodles and spread them out to cover the entire surface area. Leave untouched for 30–45 seconds, then stir-fry for 1 minute until coloured and slightly charred on the edges. Add the dark soy sauce and sugar, then stir-fry for a further 1 minute, or until the noodles are evenly coloured by the soy sauce. Transfer to a serving plate.

Add the remaining vegetable oil to the same pan, then add the tofu and spread it out evenly across the pan. Cook for 30–45 seconds on each side until nicely coloured. Once golden, add the garlic and stir-fry for 30 seconds. Add the gai lan and cook for a further 30 seconds. Pour in the stock and add all the seasoning ingredients, then stir to combine and simmer for 1–2 minutes. Gently pour in the cornflour slurry while stirring, then simmer for a further 1 minute until thickened. Spoon over the noodles and serve with the chilli vinegar, chilli flakes and chilli oil on the side. Add a little bit of everything, then mix and enjoy!

WANT TO TREAT YO' SELF? SOMETHING SPECIAL

MUM'S SMASHED STICKY PORK CHOP

PLUS MARINATING TIME

We're no gatekeepers in this family, the more the merrier and sharing is caring – well, at least I think so. Let's hope my mum agrees when she reads this. This sticky, honey-glazed, pan-seared pork chop and rice was one of my favourite dinners when I was a child, which I would always look forward to after long school days. It's my *Ratatouille* dish. Was it really that good? You be the judge.

2 x 200g pork chops
1 lemon, halved
2 tbsp vegetable oil
100g asparagus

For the marinade
½ tsp salt
½ tsp granulated sugar
½ tsp MSG
¼ tsp ground white pepper
1 tsp cornflour
1 tbsp water

For the glaze
1½ tbsp golden syrup (or honey)
1 tbsp oyster sauce
1 tsp light soy sauce
1 tbsp water

To serve
cooked jasmine rice (see page 23)
small bunch of chives, thinly sliced
Tabasco or mustard

First, slice slits into the fat of the pork chops at 2cm intervals. This will stop the pork chop from curling up when you fry it. Place the pork chops on a board and cover with a sheet of baking paper, then gently bash them with a rolling pin to flatten to 1cm thick. Transfer the chops to a bowl and add the marinade ingredients. Mix well and rub in until fully coated. If you have time, set aside to marinate for 30 minutes.

Combine the ingredients for the glaze in a bowl.

Heat a dry frying pan over a high heat, then add the lemon halves, cut side down, and cook without moving them for 2–3 minutes, or until blackened. Remove from the pan and set aside, then wipe out the pan with kitchen paper.

Heat the oil in the same frying pan over high heat. Gently place the pork chops into the pan and arrange the asparagus around the edges. Cook the chops for 1–2 minutes on each side until golden on the edges, turning the asparagus occasionally too. Remove the asparagus before flipping the chops. Once the asparagus has been removed, pour the glaze into the pan. Gently move the pan so the glaze coats the bottom of the chops. Cook for 30–45 seconds, then flip and repeat. The glaze should stick to the pork and caramelise.

Spoon the rice onto plates and lean the chops on the rice. Add the asparagus, sprinkle with chives and finish with a burnt lemon half. Add a few drops of Tabasco or mustard and enjoy!

THAI BASIL AND CHILLI PRAWNS

This one is not for the faint hearted . . . seriously, I'm not joking! The chilli and garlic might seem like overkill, but once they touch the pan the flavours mellow out. The whole thing is cooked in minutes, so need I say more?

2 tbsp vegetable oil
4 Thai chillies, very finely chopped
4 garlic cloves, very finely chopped
1 shallot, diced
1 tbsp Thai chilli paste (I use Mae Ploy)
½ tsp granulated sugar
1 tsp fish sauce
1 tbsp oyster sauce
200g cooked or raw peeled king prawns, butterflied
1–2 tbsp water
small bunch of Thai basil (or regular basil), leaves picked

To serve
cooked jasmine rice (see page 23)
lime wedges

Heat a large wok or frying pan over a high heat for 1–2 minutes, then add the oil, followed by the chilli, garlic and shallot. Stir-fry for 1 minute until fragrant. Add the chilli paste and sugar and fry for a further 30 seconds, then add fish sauce and oyster sauce and stir. Add the prawns and stir-fry until cooked, 1–2 minutes if raw and just 30–45 seconds if cooked. Add the water and cook for a further 1 minute, then remove from the heat and fold through the basil leaves.

Divide the rice between shallow bowls and spoon the prawns over the top. Garnish with a wedge of lime.

CRISPY CHICKEN WITH SCORCHED GINGER-CHILLI SAUCE

Featuring one of the most addictive sauces you'll ever try, this dish has a bit of added drama included as you scorch the aromatics with hot oil. It really makes the sauce the star of the show! You want the oil to be smoking hot before you pour it over – don't worry, it won't burn anything. The key to crispy chicken thighs is starting with a cold pan and no oil. This ensures that as much fat as possible renders from the skin! Don't touch it, let it do its thing and trust the process!

1 thumb-sized piece of fresh ginger
small bunch of coriander
2 spring onions
4 garlic cloves, finely chopped
2 bird's eye chillies
4 tbsp vegetable oil
juice of 1 lime
1 tbsp rice vinegar
1 tbsp sriracha
1 tsp granulated sugar
1 tbsp dark soy sauce
225g jasmine rice
340ml chicken stock
4 skin-on boneless chicken thighs
salt

Slice off two thin slices of ginger and then cut them into thin matchsticks and set aside. Roughly chop the rest. Thinly slice a quarter of the coriander and set it aside too. Cut one of the spring onions in half to separate the white and the green parts. Thinly slice the green part and set it aside with the sliced coriander.

Cut the white part of the spring onion in half lengthways, then slice it as thinly as possible into matchsticks. Roughly chop the remaining coriander. Put the spring onion matchsticks and chopped coriander into a bowl of ice-cold water.

Add half the garlic, the chillies and the chopped ginger to a mortar and pestle and bash for 1 minute until a chunky consistency. Add the reserved spring onion greens, sliced coriander and a pinch of salt.

Heat 3 tablespoons of the oil in a small frying pan over high heat for about 3 minutes until smoking, then carefully pour the hot oil into the mortar to scorch the aromatics. Add half the lime juice, the rice vinegar, sriracha, sugar and dark soy sauce. Stir well to combine.

Put the rice into a bowl and cover with cold water. Rinse the rice and then pour out the water. Repeat this twice, or until the water is clear, then drain.

Heat the remaining 1 tablespoon of oil in a saucepan over medium heat, then add the remaining chopped garlic, ginger matchsticks and remaining whole spring onion and stir-fry for 1 minute. Add the rice, a pinch of salt and the chicken stock. Stir once to combine, then cover, increase the heat to high and bring to the boil. As soon as the water is at a rolling boil, reduce the heat to the lowest setting. Cook for 18 minutes without removing the lid. After this time, remove the pan from the heat and set aside, covered, until you're ready to serve.

Dab the chicken skin with kitchen paper to remove as much moisture as possible, then season with a generous pinch of salt. Place the chicken thighs into a cold frying pan, skin side down. Turn the heat to medium. Don't touch or move the chicken – this ensures the skin stays crispy and helps to render the fat. Cook for 7 minutes, then flip and cook the other side for a further 3 minutes. Remove and set aside to rest for 5 minutes.

Slice the chicken into roughly 1cm strips, using one smooth action and the weight of the knife to keep the skin attached to the meat.

Divide the rice between plates, then top with the chicken. Generously spoon over the sauce, using the back of the spoon to spread it over evenly. Drain the water from the spring onion and coriander, add a pinch of salt and a squeeze of lime juice and mix well, then divide between the plates to finish.

(See photo overleaf)

ROASTED MISO COD

A good-quality, fresh fillet of fish needs very little to make it bang. A simple miso and mirin marinade that is brushed on the fish before baking in the oven is the perfect addition. Less is more. The key is to wipe the excess marinade off before cooking, which allows the sweet miso to slightly burn. Serve with a bowl of steaming rice and a zingy onion side salad.

1½ tbsp miso paste
1 tbsp granulated sugar
2 tbsp mirin
2 x 150g cod loin fillets
1 tbsp vegetable oil

For the onion salad
1 onion, thinly sliced
juice of 1 lemon
1 tbsp rice vinegar
2 tbsp light soy sauce
1 tsp sesame oil
small bunch of chives, thinly sliced
1 tbsp sesame seeds

To serve
cooked Japanese short-grain rice (see page 23)
lemon wedges

Combine the miso paste, sugar and mirin in a shallow dish and whisk until the sugar has dissolved. Add the cod and cover in the marinade. Leave to sit for at least 30 minutes or, even better, overnight.

When you're ready to cook, preheat the oven to 220°C/200°C fan/gas mark 7.

To prepare the onion salad, combine the onion, lemon juice, vinegar, soy sauce and sesame oil in a bowl and then set aside while you bake the fish.

Using your fingers, gently scrape the marinade off the fish – just a few streaks and a thin layer of miso is what we're looking for. Brush a baking tray with the oil and place the fillets on top. Cook in the oven for 15 minutes, or until the edges have blackened. Remove and leave to rest for 3 minutes.

Drain the liquid from the onions and then add the chives and sesame seeds. Mix to combine.

Place the cod on plates along with the onion salad and garnish with a lemon wedge. Serve with the rice.

GARLIC BUTTER CRISPY CHICKEN RICE

Decadent, crispy, garlic butter-soaked chicken, made without the stress of deep-frying. This shallow-fried chicken is dusted with a light coating of cornflour, which locks in the seasonings to keep the chicken extra juicy! It's paired with a concentrated sweet soy sauce that soaks into every single grain of rice. Inspired by the Korean and Japanese obsession with fried chicken, the boneless bite-sized pieces cut the cooking time in half. To add indulgence, throw an egg yolk on top and dip in a piece of chicken before you eat!

8 tbsp light soy sauce
8 tbsp mirin
2 tbsp light brown soft sugar
4 tbsp unsalted butter
4 cloves of garlic, very finely chopped
1 tbsp chilli powder
zest of 1 lemon
large bunch of chives, sliced
4 skinless and boneless chicken thighs, cut into bite-sized pieces
1 thumb-sized piece of fresh ginger, grated
4 tbsp cornflour
200ml oil, or as needed
2 medium egg yolks
salt and freshly ground black pepper
cooked short-grain rice (see page 23), to serve

Put 6 tablespoons of the soy sauce, 6 tablespoons of the mirin and the brown sugar into a small saucepan. Heat over a medium heat for 5 minutes, or until reduced by a third. Transfer to a small jug and set aside.

Melt the butter in a small saucepan over a medium heat, then add a third of the garlic and stir for 30 seconds. Add another third and stir for a further 30 seconds, then repeat with the remaining garlic.

Put the chilli powder, a pinch of salt, the lemon zest and three quarters of the chives into a large bowl and pour over the garlic butter. Stir to combine.

In a separate bowl, combine the chicken with the ginger, the remaining 2 tablespoons of soy sauce and mirin, a big pinch of salt and pepper, and mix thoroughly. Add the cornflour and toss until the chicken is coated.

Heat the oil in a frying pan over a medium-high heat for about 3 minutes. It should be 1–2cm deep, so add more if you need to. Carefully place the chicken in the pan and gently push the pieces apart to prevent them from sticking. Cook for 5 minutes, then flip the pieces and cook for a further 5 minutes. Remove from the pan and toss in the garlic butter.

Put the rice into bowls and top with the fried chicken. Push the chicken towards the edge to make a small well in the centre and add an egg yolk. Sprinkle with the remaining chives. Pour the sauce over the chicken and enjoy.

GARLIC BUTTER SALMON FRIED RICE

Fried rice always calls to me after a long day out, but this is no regular fried rice. What people don't know is that fried rice can be elevated to a well-rounded, luxurious meal, just like instant noodles. In this version, flaked salmon fillets, rice and garlic butter are tossed together and then finished with lots of chives and lemon. This is one of the easiest midweek staples you can learn!

1 tbsp vegetable oil
2 x 120g salmon fillets (with or without skin)
1½ tbsp unsalted butter
5 garlic cloves, sliced
300g cooked Japanese short-grain rice (see page 23)
2 medium eggs
1 tbsp sesame seeds
1 tsp freshly ground black pepper
½ tsp ground white pepper
1 tbsp light soy sauce
1 tsp fish sauce
1 tsp MSG
1 tsp sesame oil
pinch of salt, or to taste
small bunch of chives, sliced
lemon wedges, to serve

Heat a wok or large frying pan over a medium-high heat for 1–2 minutes, then pour in the oil and place the salmon fillets in the pan skin side down (if skinless, lay on either side). Fry for 3 minutes, then flip and cook for a further 3 minutes. Transfer the fillets to a plate, then use your fingers to remove the skin. It should peel off easily. With a fork, gently flake the fish into large chunks.

Add 1 tablespoon of the butter and the sliced garlic to the same pan and cook for 1 minute, or until the garlic has turned golden brown, but not burnt. Add the rice and use a spatula or spoon to gently bash the clumps of rice to separate the grains. Push the rice to one side, then add the remaining butter and crack in the eggs. Scramble until marbled and slightly cooked. Push the rice on top of the eggs, add the flaked salmon and stir until fully combined. Season with the black pepper, white pepper, soy sauce, fish sauce, MSG, sesame oil and salt. Fry for a further 3–5 minutes, stirring and tossing constantly. Finally, add the sesame seeds and chopped chives and stir to combine.

Transfer to serving bowls and serve with a wedge of lemon.

MACKEREL CURRY AND RICE

PREP TIME 5 MINUTES
SERVES 1
COOK TIME 15 MINUTES

All too often, chicken curry takes the limelight but, in my honest opinion, fish curry is the real winner. Any rich and oily fish pairs perfectly with a spicy, coconut cream base (the creamier, thicker and sweeter cousin of coconut milk). Using shop-bought curry paste makes this a seriously easy recipe that will still impress your guest. Save a little coconut cream to drizzle over the top at the end, then top with fresh chilli and basil and serve with fragrant jasmine rice.

1 tbsp red curry paste (I use Mae Ploy)
400ml coconut cream
1 tsp granulated sugar
splash of fish sauce, if needed
2 skin-on mackerel fillets
pinch of salt
1 tbsp vegetable oil
small bunch of chives, thinly sliced
½ red chilli, thinly sliced
small bunch of Thai basil (or regular basil), leaves picked
wedge of lime
cooked jasmine rice (see page 23), to serve

Combine the curry paste and 100ml of the coconut cream in a small saucepan over a high heat and stir until fully combined. Cook for 2–3 minutes, or until the liquid has reduced and the oil starts to split, then add the sugar and the remaining coconut cream, reserving 2 tablespoons to drizzle on at the end. Cook for a further 2-3 minutes. Check the seasoning – it should be salty and sweet, but adjust with a splash of fish sauce if needed. Remove from the heat and set aside.

Score the skin of the mackerel in 2cm intervals, then very lightly season the skin with the salt.

Heat the oil in a frying pan over a medium-high heat for 1–2 minutes, then gently place the mackerel fillets into the pan, skin side down. The skin will curl up immediately, so use your fingers to press down for 30 seconds so that it flattens. Cook for 3 minutes until the skin is golden and crispy, then flip over and remove from the heat.

Pour the curry sauce into a wide, shallow bowl and sprinkle over the chives and chilli. Place the mackerel fillets on top of the curry, skin side up. Garnish with the Thai basil and a wedge of lime. Enjoy with rice.

THINLY SLICED RARE STEAK RICE BOWL

PREP TIME 5 MINUTES · SERVES 2 · COOK TIME 8 MINUTES

Inspired by my love for Japanese donburi, or rice bowls, this thinly sliced steak bowl seriously hits the spot! Steaming rice is topped with shredded lettuce, Japanese mayonnaise, steak – of course – and a sweet onion and soy dressing that saturates the rice. My tip for shredding the lettuce: roll the leaves up into a cigar shape and then thinly slice. Optional, but recommended, is a raw egg yolk on top to make it really luxurious.

400g sirloin steak
1 tbsp vegetable oil
1 tbsp unsalted butter
1 garlic clove, peeled but left whole
2 tbsp mirin
2 tbsp light soy sauce
½ tsp dashi powder (optional)
½ onion, grated
squeeze of lemon juice
3 iceberg lettuce leaves, thinly sliced
3 tbsp Japanese mayonnaise, such as Kewpie
small bunch of chives, thinly sliced
2 medium egg yolks (optional)
salt and freshly ground black pepper
cooked Japanese short-grain rice (see page 23), to serve

Season the steak all over with a pinch of salt and black pepper.

Heat a dry frying pan over a high heat for 2–3 minutes, or until smoking, then add the oil. Gently place the steak into the pan and fry for 1–2 minutes on each side for medium-rare, or cook to your preference. In the last minute of cooking, add the butter and whole garlic clove. Use a spoon to baste the butter on top of the steak, then lower the heat to medium, remove the steak and set aside to rest for 5 minutes. Don't wipe out the pan.

Add the mirin to the pan, followed by the light soy sauce, dashi powder (if using), grated onion and a squeeze of lemon juice. Stir to combine. Remove from the heat and pour into a bowl.

Once the steak has rested, slice it as thinly as possible.

Divide the rice between bowls and top with the shredded lettuce. Drizzle or dollop on the mayonnaise to cover the lettuce, then arrange the steak slices on the lettuce in a flower or fan shape. Generously sprinkle with chives.

Using your finger, make a small well in the centre of each mound of steak and place an egg yolk on top (if using). Generously spoon the sauce onto the steak and serve.

FRIED FISH BASIL CURRY

PREP TIME 10 MINUTES
SERVES 2
COOK TIME 20 MINUTES

Curry sauce has become a staple in chippies across the UK and rightly so! Here, British chippy meets Thai flavours, with battered fish covered in a red curry sauce marbled with coconut milk. Curry pastes are a great addition to the kitchen as they're used as a base for many dishes, but there always seems to be a bit left over that ends up hanging around in the back of the fridge. This is one of my all-time favourite ways to use up the rest of that jar.

200g self-raising flour
2 tbsp cornflour
1 tsp salt
1 medium egg, beaten
300ml cold water
500ml vegetable oil, or as needed
300g cod loin, cut into 7–10cm pieces
cooked jasmine rice (see page 23), to serve

For the curry sauce
1 tbsp vegetable oil
½ banana shallot, diced
1 garlic clove, finely chopped
1 thick slice ginger, finely choped
1 tbsp red curry paste (I use Mae Ploy)
400ml coconut milk
½ tsp fish sauce
½ tsp granulated sugar
½ red chilli, thinly sliced
small bunch of Thai basil leaves

Combine the flour, cornflour and salt in a bowl and stir well to combine. Whisk together the egg and water in a jug, then pour the mixture into the flour and whisk until combined into a smooth batter. Let the batter sit while you make the curry sauce.

Heat the oil in a saucepan over a medium-high heat for 1 minute, then add the shallot, garlic and ginger and fry for 1–2 minutes. Add the curry paste and stir to combine, then fry for a further 1 minute. Pour in the coconut milk, reserving 2 tablespoons to serve. Add the fish sauce and sugar and bring to the boil, then reduce the heat to medium and simmer for 4–6 minutes, or until the sauce has reduced by half. Remove from the heat and stir in the chilli and Thai basil. Set aside.

Heat at least 8cm oil in a large saucepan over a medium-high heat until it reaches 175°C. To test the oil, hold a chopstick in the pan. If bubbles rapidly form around the chopstick, the oil is ready.

While the oil is heating, place the fish in the batter and coat it on all sides. One by one, lower the pieces of fish into the hot oil. Cook for 2–3 minutes on each side until golden and crispy. Remove the fish with a slotted spoon and drain on kitchen paper.

Place the fish on plates and pour over the curry sauce. Drizzle with the reserved coconut milk and marble it into the sauce. Enjoy with a plate of steaming hot rice.

MISO BUTTER PORK CHOP AND POTATO SALAD

PREP TIME 10 MINUTES
SERVES 2
COOK TIME 30 MINUTES

Have you ever tried Japanese potato salad? It's similar to the iconic Western barbecue side dish but includes carrot, cucumber, egg and sweetcorn. It's also tangier and crunchier and, hand on heart, I think it's better in every way! Served with a seared pork chop drizzled with umami-rich miso butter, what could be better?

2 x 200g pork chops
2 tbsp vegetable oil
2 tbsp unsalted butter
2 tbsp white miso paste
2 tbsp mirin
2 tsp granulated sugar
zest and juice of 1 lemon
bunch of chives, chopped
salt and freshly ground black pepper

For the potato salad
2 large potatoes, peeled and quartered
½ carrot, thinly sliced
2 medium eggs
¼ cucumber, thinly sliced
½ x 200g tin of sweetcorn, drained
1 tbsp rice vinegar
1 tsp freshly ground black pepper
3 tbsp Japanese mayonnaise, such as Kewpie
salt

First, make the potato salad. Put the potatoes into a saucepan with a teaspoon of salt and cover with water, then bring to the boil and cook for 15 minutes. Drain and place in a large bowl, then lightly mash the potato into small chunks with a fork or potato masher. Set aside to cool.

Bring a saucepan of water to the boil and cook the carrot for 5 minutes, drain and set aside. Using the same pan, boil the eggs for 12 minutes, then drain and refresh under cold water. Once cool, peel and chop.

Add the carrot and egg to the bowl with the potato, then add all the remaining ingredients for the salad, season with salt and stir to combine.

Slice slits into the fat of the pork chop at 2cm intervals. This will stop the pork chop from curling up when you fry it. Season with salt and pepper on both sides.

Heat a dry frying pan over a high heat for 1–2 minutes, then add the oil and swirl the pan so that the oil coats the base. Gently place the pork chop into the pan and cook for 2–3 minutes on each side. Remove the chop and leave it to rest while you make the miso butter.

Add the butter to the same pan over a medium heat, then add the miso paste, mirin, sugar and lemon zest and juice and whisk to combine. Cook for 1 minute, or until the sauce has started to bubble. Remove from the heat and stir in the chives.

Place the pork chop onto a plate followed by the potato salad. Spoon the miso butter over the pork chop and enjoy!

COOK'S NOTES

1. Fruits and vegetables are assumed to be medium sized and washed, unless specified otherwise.

2. Onions, garlic, ginger and avocados are assumed to be peeled.

3. Meat and eggs should be high-welfare and free-range where possible.

4. When using the zest of citrus fruit, buy unwaxed.

5. Some recipes include raw or lightly cooked eggs, meat or fish. Care should be taken when consuming these ingredients, especially for children, pregnant women or anyone with an impaired immune system.

6. When no quantity is specified, for example of oils, salts and herbs used for finishing dishes or frying, quantities are discretionary and flexible.

7. When no type or weight is specified for instant noodles, the choice is yours.

CONVERSIONS

The recipes in this book have been tested using metric measurements.
Follow one set of measurements only – do not mix metric and imperial.

WEIGHT

Metric	Imperial
15g	½oz
25g	1oz
40g	1½oz
50g	2oz
75g	3oz
100g	4oz
150g	5oz
175g	6oz
200g	7oz
225g	8oz
250g	9oz
275g	10oz
350g	12oz
375g	13oz
400g	14oz
425g	15oz
450g	1lb
550g	1¼lb
675g	1½lb
900g	2lb
1.5kg	3lb
1.75kg	4lb
2.25kg	5lb

LIQUID VOLUME

Metric	Imperial
25ml	1fl oz
50ml	2fl oz
85ml	3fl oz
150 ml	5fl oz (¼ pint)
300 ml	10fl oz (½ pint)
450 ml	15fl oz (¾ pint)
600 ml	1 pint
700 ml	1¼ pints
900 ml	1½ pints
1 litre	1¾ pints
1.2 litres	2 pints
1.25 litres	2¼ pints
1.5 litres	2½ pints
1.6 litres	2¾ pints
1.75 litres	3 pints
1.8 litres	3¼ pints
2 litres	3½ pints
2.1 litres	3¾ pints
2.25 litres	4 pints
2.75 litres	5 pints
3.4 litres	6 pints
3.9 litres	7 pints
5 litres	8 pints (1 gallon)

MEASUREMENTS

Metric	Imperial
0.5cm	¼ inch
1cm	½ inch
2.5cm	1 inch
5cm	2 inches
7.5cm	3 inches
10cm	4 inches
15cm	6 inches
18cm	7 inches
20cm	8 inches
23cm	9 inches
25cm	10 inches
30cm	12 inches

OVEN TEMPERATURES

°C	Fan °C	°F	Gas Mark
140°C	120°C	140°F	Gas Mark 1
150°C	130°C	150°F	Gas Mark 2
160°C	140°C	160°F	Gas Mark 3
180°C	160°C	180°F	Gas Mark 4
190°C	170°C	190°F	Gas Mark 5
200°C	180°C	200°F	Gas Mark 6
220°C	200°C	220°F	Gas Mark 7
230°C	210°C	230°F	Gas Mark 8
240°C	220°C	240°F	Gas Mark 9

INDEX

anti-hanger peanut butter chilli oil noodles 88
asparagus: crispy noodles with prawn, asparagus and mushroom sauce 154

bacon: bacon and kimchi fried rice, nori, mayo and chilli burnt corn and crispy fried egg 65
bangers and tomato rice 47
carbonara instant noodles 93
creamy baked prawn rice 43
peanut butter bacon French toast 34
bake, gochujang prawn pasta 107
bangers and tomato rice 47
beans: white bean and leek miso soup 114
beansprout salad, spicy 197
beef: braised minced beef with crispy fried leeks and eggs 160
coriander chutney beef tataki 124
garlic beef udon soup 78
ginger and onion rib-eye steak 141
ginger chilli beef udon 67
herby lime steak and pickled onions 82
Parmesan, herb and chilli beef salad 74
sizzling beef pepper rice with honey-garlic sauce 184
spicy miso beef udon soup 172
steak sando 180
thinly sliced rare steak rice bowl 225
thinly sliced steak with citrus sauce 182
bread: crispy chicken katsu sando 188–9
five-spice salt and pepper squid baguette 207
peanut butter bacon French toast 34
breakfast baps, HK-style 44
brioche: chicken teriyaki brioche burger 175
fish finger sando 37
HK-style breakfast bap 44
peanut butter bacon French toast 34
steak sando 180
burgers, chicken teriyaki brioche 175

cabbage: braised cabbage and garlic noodles 97
coriander and mint slaw 122
spicy miso grilled cabbage 104
Caesar salad, grilled cumin chicken and herb 137
carbonara instant noodles 93
celery and coriander salad 151
ceviche, ginger-soy 113
cheat's prawn and cucumber laksa 208
cheese: carbonara instant noodles 93
cheese and Spam instant noodle hotpot 102
Parmesan, herb and chilli beef salad 74
chicken: baked honey and sesame chicken 122
chicken and mushroom claypot rice 157
chicken and mushroom lettuce cups 131–2
chicken and sweetcorn rice 196
chicken teriyaki brioche burger 175
chicken thigh and honey gochujang instant noodles 68
chilli butter chicken with fennel salad 77
coriander and lime butter drumsticks 151
crispy chicken katsu sando 188–9
crispy chicken with scorched ginger-chilli sauce 214–15
firecracker rice 109
fish sauce chicken wings 178
Fujian fried rice with chicken, prawn and Chinese sausage 194
garlic butter crispy chicken rice 221
grilled cumin chicken and herb Caesar salad 137
honey-roasted cumin chicken with sesame rice 162–3
kimchi and garlic chicken quesadillas 85
lemongrass chicken with herb salad 138
marbled eggs and chicken over rice 50
poached chicken gravy rice 153
sake grilled wings with salt and lime 118
saucy braised chicken noodles 197
shredded chicken noodle salad 116
soy-glazed chicken and chive rice bowl 81
spicy and sour soup noodles 91
spicy chicken escalope sando 70–1
sweet braised chicken and mushroom rice 152
tangy instant noodle salad 121
triple garlic crispy chicken 128
volcano chilli chicken 193
chilli oil: anti-hanger peanut butter chilli oil noodles 88
five-minute chilli oil udon 58
chillies: bacon and kimchi fried rice, nori, mayo and chilli burnt corn and crispy fried egg 65

232

chilli and onion salsa 68
chilli and sesame dumpling salad 95
chilli butter chicken with fennel salad 77
chilli cucumber pickle 123
crispy chicken with scorched ginger-chilli sauce 214–15
ginger chilli beef udon 67
Parmesan, herb and chilli beef salad 74
quick-pickled chillies 159
Thai basil and chilli prawns 212
volcano chilli chicken 193
Chinese sausage, Fujian fried rice with chicken, prawn and 194
chorizo: spicy miso grilled cabbage 104
chutney, coriander 124
citrus sauce, thinly sliced steak with 182
claypot rice: chicken and mushroom claypot rice 157
sesame ginger salmon claypot rice 53
cod: fried fish basil curry 226
roasted miso cod 219
cream cheese salmon sushi tacos 146
creamy baked prawn rice 43
creamy gochujang prawn noodles 39
crispy chicken katsu sando 188–9
crispy chicken with scorched ginger-chilli sauce 214–15
crispy garlic pork belly bites 145
crispy noodles with prawn, asparagus and mushroom sauce 154
cucumber: cheat's prawn and cucumber laksa 208
cucumber pickles 123, 166, 188–9

five-minute chilli oil udon with cucumber and coriander 58
smashed cucumber 61
curry: curry egg udon 66
fried fish basil curry 226
mackerel curry and rice 223
spring onion pancakes with curry sauce 26

dumplings: chilli and sesame dumpling salad 95
dumpling soup noodles 40

eggs: bacon and kimchi fried rice, nori, mayo and chilli burnt corn and crispy fried egg 65
braised minced beef with crispy fried leeks and eggs 160
carbonara instant noodles 93
curry egg udon 66
egg yolk mayo instant noodles 90
green eggs and rice 29
HK-style breakfast bap 44
kimchi egg ribbon udon soup 99
marbled eggs and chicken over rice 50
peanut butter bacon French toast 34
sesame ginger salmon claypot rice 53
shiitake mushroom and coriander egg drop soup 59
soy-glazed chicken and chive rice bowl 81
sweet soy scrambled eggs 32
twenty-clove garlic noodles 96

fennel salad 77
firecracker rice 109

fish: cream cheese salmon sushi tacos 146
fish finger sando 37
fried fish basil curry 226
garlic butter salmon bites 123
garlic butter salmon fried rice 222
grilled cumin chicken and herb Caesar salad 137
mackerel curry and rice 223
miso baked salmon with grilled spring onions 134
roasted miso cod 219
seared sea bass and onion salad 127
sesame ginger salmon claypot rice 53
fish sauce chicken wings 178
five-minute chilli oil udon 58
five-spice salt and pepper squid baguette 207
French toast, peanut butter bacon 34
Fujian fried rice with chicken, prawn and Chinese sausage 194

garlic: braised cabbage and garlic noodles 97
crispy garlic pork belly bites 145
garlic beef udon soup 78
garlic butter crispy chicken rice 221
garlic butter salmon bites 123
garlic butter salmon fried rice 222
kimchi and garlic chicken quesadillas 85
sizzling beef pepper rice with honey-garlic sauce 184
spicy garlic butter udon 61
sticky ginger and garlic ribs 204
triple garlic crispy chicken 128
twenty-clove garlic noodles 96
ginger: crispy chicken with scorched ginger-chilli sauce 214–15

ginger and onion rib-eye steak 141
ginger chilli beef udon 67
ginger-soy ceviche 113
sesame ginger salmon claypot rice 53
sticky ginger and garlic ribs 204
gochujang 16
  chicken thigh and honey gochujang instant noodles 68
  creamy gochujang prawn noodles 39
  gochujang prawn pasta bake 107
gravy: chopped roast pork gravy rice 198–201
green beans: spicy green bean and tofu stew 148
green eggs and rice 29

ham: sweet soy scrambled eggs 32
herbs: green eggs and rice 29
  grilled cumin chicken and herb Caesar salad 137
  herby salad 82
  lemongrass chicken with herb salad 138
  Parmesan, herb and chilli beef salad 74
  prawn and herb salad 48
  triple garlic crispy chicken with green rice and sauce 128
HK-style breakfast bap 44
ho fun, fried tofu 210
honey: baked honey and sesame chicken 122
  chicken thigh and honey gochujang instant noodles 68
  honey-roasted cumin chicken with sesame rice 162–3
  sizzling beef pepper rice with honey-garlic sauce 184
hotpot, cheese and Spam instant noodle 102

ingredients 14–23

katsu: crispy chicken katsu sando 188–9
kimchi: bacon and kimchi fried rice, nori, mayo and chilli burnt corn and crispy fried egg 65
  kimchi and garlic chicken quesadillas with chive butter 85
  kimchi egg ribbon udon soup 99
  kimchi pork belly 166

laksa, cheat's prawn and cucumber 208
lamb: cumin and potato braised leg of lamb 169
  tender braised lamb with quick-pickled chillies 159
leeks: braised minced beef with crispy fried leeks and eggs 160
  white bean and leek miso soup 114
lemongrass chicken with herb salad 138
lettuce: chicken and mushroom lettuce cups 131–2
  grilled cumin chicken and herb Caesar salad 137
limes: coriander and lime butter drumsticks 151
  lime mayonnaise 82
  sake grilled wings with salt and lime 118
  spicy lime sauce 187

marbled eggs and chicken over rice 50
mayonnaise 16
  bacon and kimchi fried rice, nori, mayo and chilli burnt corn and crispy fried egg 65
  egg yolk mayo instant noodles 90
miso: miso baked salmon with grilled spring onions 134
  miso butter pork chop and potato salad 228
  miso mushroom udon 56
  roasted miso cod 219

spicy miso beef udon soup 172
spicy miso grilled cabbage 104
white bean and leek miso soup 114
Mum's smashed sticky pork chop 211
mushrooms: chicken and mushroom claypot rice 157
  chicken and mushroom lettuce cups 131–2
  crispy noodles with prawn, asparagus and mushroom sauce 154
  miso mushroom udon 56
  shiitake mushroom and coriander egg drop soup 59
  sweet braised chicken and mushroom rice 152

noodles 16
  anti-hanger peanut butter chilli oil noodles 88
  baked black pepper prawn glass noodles 187
  braised cabbage and garlic noodles 97
  burnt spring onion udon 100
  carbonara instant noodles 93
  cheat's prawn and cucumber laksa 208
  cheese and Spam instant noodle hotpot 102
  chicken thigh and honey gochujang instant noodles 68
  creamy gochujang prawn noodles 39
  crispy noodles with prawn, asparagus and mushroom sauce 154
  curry egg udon 66
  dumpling soup noodles 40
  egg yolk mayo instant noodles 90
  five-minute chilli oil udon with cucumber and coriander 58
  garlic beef udon soup 78
  ginger chilli beef udon 67
  kimchi egg ribbon udon soup 99

miso mushroom udon 56
saucy braised chicken noodles 197
shredded chicken noodle salad 116
spicy and sour soup noodles 91
spicy braised pork saucy
   noodles 158
spicy garlic butter udon 61
spicy miso beef udon soup 172
tangy instant noodle salad 121
triple-threat spring onion
   noodles 33
twenty-clove garlic noodles 96
udon noodles 19
nori 17
   bacon and kimchi fried rice, nori,
     mayo and chilli burnt corn and
     crispy fried egg 65

onions: chilli and onion salsa 68
   ginger and onion rib-eye steak 141
   onion salad 219
   pickled onions 82, 131–2
   seared sea bass and onion salad 127
   soy onions 166

pasta bake, gochujang prawn 107
peanut butter: anti-hanger peanut
   butter chilli oil noodles 88
   peanut butter bacon French
     toast 34
pickles: cucumber pickles 123, 166,
   188–9
   pickled onions 82, 131–2
   quick-pickled chillies 159
pork: chopped roast pork gravy rice
   198–201
   crispy garlic pork belly bites 145
   kimchi pork belly 166
   miso butter pork chop and potato
     salad 228
   Mum's smashed sticky pork
     chop 211
   spicy braised pork saucy
     noodles 158

spicy pork baked potato 183
sticky ginger and garlic ribs 204
potatoes: cumin and potato braised
   leg of lamb 169
   potato salad 228
   spicy pork baked potato 183
prawns: baked black pepper prawn
   glass noodles 187
   cheat's prawn and cucumber
     laksa 208
   creamy baked prawn rice 43
   creamy gochujang prawn
     noodles 39
   crispy noodles with prawn,
     asparagus and mushroom
     sauce 154
   Fujian fried rice with chicken,
     prawn and Chinese sausage 194
   ginger-soy ceviche 113
   gochujang prawn pasta bake 107
   prawn and herb salad 48
   Thai basil and chilli prawns 212

quesadillas, kimchi and garlic
   chicken 85

rice 20–3
   bacon and kimchi fried rice, nori,
     mayo and chilli burnt corn and
     crispy fried egg 65
   bangers and tomato rice 47
   chicken and mushroom claypot
     rice 157
   chicken and sweetcorn rice 196
   chopped roast pork gravy rice
     198–201
   cream cheese salmon sushi
     tacos 146
   creamy baked prawn rice 43
   crispy chicken with scorched
     ginger-chilli sauce 214–15
   firecracker rice 109
   Fujian fried rice with chicken,
     prawn and Chinese sausage 194

garlic butter crispy chicken rice 221
garlic butter salmon fried rice 222
green eggs and rice 29
honey-roasted cumin chicken with
   sesame rice 162–3
mackerel curry and rice 223
marbled eggs and chicken over
   rice 50
poached chicken gravy rice 153
sesame ginger salmon claypot
   rice 53
sizzling beef pepper rice 184
soy-glazed chicken and chive
   rice bowl 81
sweet braised chicken and
   mushroom rice 152
thinly sliced rare steak rice bowl 225
triple garlic crispy chicken with
   green rice and sauce 128

sake grilled wings with salt and
   lime 118
salads: celery and coriander salad 151
   chilli and sesame dumpling salad 95
   chilli butter chicken with fennel
     salad 77
   coriander and mint slaw 122
   grilled cumin chicken and herb
     Caesar salad 137
   herb salad 82
   lemongrass chicken with herb
     salad 138
   onion salad 219
   Parmesan, herb and chilli
     beef salad 74
   potato salad 228
   prawn and herb salad 48
   seared sea bass and onion salad 127
   shredded chicken noodle salad 116
   spicy beansprout salad 197
   spicy sesame green salad 115
   spring onion salad 166
   tangy instant noodle salad 121
salsa, chilli and onion 68

sandwiches/sandos: crispy chicken katsu sando 188–9
fish finger sando with lime, wasabi and chive mayo 37
five-spice salt and pepper squid baguette 207
HK-style breakfast bap 44
spicy chicken escalope sando 70–1
steak sando 180
saucy braised chicken noodles with spicy beansprout salad 197
sausages: bangers and tomato rice 47
cheese and Spam instant noodle hotpot 102
Fujian fried rice with chicken, prawn and Chinese sausage 194
sesame seeds: baked honey and sesame chicken with coriander and mint slaw 122
chilli and sesame dumpling salad 95
honey-roasted cumin chicken with sesame rice 162–3
sesame ginger salmon claypot rice 53
spicy sesame green salad 115
sizzling beef pepper rice with honey-garlic sauce 184
slaw, coriander and mint 122
soups: cheat's prawn and cucumber laksa 208
dumpling soup noodles 40
garlic beef udon soup 78
kimchi egg ribbon udon soup 99
shiitake mushroom and coriander egg drop soup 59
spicy and sour soup noodles 91
spicy miso beef udon soup 172
white bean and leek miso soup 114
soy sauce: ginger-soy ceviche 113
soy-glazed chicken and chive rice bowl 81
soy onions 166
sweet soy scrambled eggs 32

Spam: cheese and Spam instant noodle hotpot 102
HK-style breakfast bap 44
spicy and sour soup noodles 91
spicy braised pork saucy noodles 158
spicy chicken escalope sando 70–1
spicy garlic butter udon with smashed cucumber 61
spicy green bean and tofu stew 148
spicy miso beef udon soup 172
spicy miso grilled cabbage 104
spicy pork baked potato 183
spicy sesame green salad 115
spring onions: burnt spring onion udon 100
miso baked salmon with grilled spring onions 134
spring onion pancakes with curry sauce 26
spring onion salad 166
triple-threat spring onion noodles 33
squid: five-spice salt and pepper squid baguette 207
stew, spicy green bean and tofu 148
sticky ginger and garlic ribs 204
sushi: cream cheese salmon sushi tacos 146
sweet braised chicken and mushroom rice 152
sweet soy scrambled eggs 32
sweetcorn: bacon and kimchi fried rice, nori, mayo and chilli burnt corn and crispy fried egg 65
chicken and sweetcorn rice 196

tacos, cream cheese salmon sushi 146
tangy instant noodle salad 121
tataki, coriander chutney beef 124
teriyaki: chicken teriyaki brioche burger 175
tofu: braised cabbage and garlic noodles 97
cheese and Spam instant noodle hotpot 102

fried tofu ho fun 210
shiitake mushroom and coriander egg drop soup 59
spicy green bean and tofu stew 148
tomatoes: bangers and tomato rice 47
tortilla wraps: kimchi and garlic chicken quesadillas 85
triple garlic crispy chicken with green rice and sauce 128
triple-threat spring onion noodles 33
twenty-clove garlic noodles 96

udon noodles *see* noodles

vegetarian: anti-hanger peanut butter chilli oil noodles 88
burnt spring onion udon 100
chilli and sesame dumpling salad 95
curry egg udon 66
egg yolk mayo instant noodles 90
five-minute chilli oil udon with cucumber and coriander 58
fried tofu ho fun 210
kimchi egg ribbon udon soup 99
miso mushroom udon 56
shiitake mushroom and coriander egg drop soup 59
spicy garlic butter udon with smashed cucumber 61
spicy green bean and tofu stew 148
spicy sesame green salad 115
spring onion pancakes with curry sauce 26
triple-threat spring onion noodles 33
white bean and leek miso soup 114
volcano chilli chicken 193

ABOUT THE AUTHOR

Justin 'Dustbin' Tsang is a cook specialising in indulgent, home-cooked Asian food with a twist. Inspired by his upbringing around his parents' Chinese restaurants, he shares his knowledge on cooking techniques and making Asian cooking more exciting and accessible. He lives in London and can be found on Instagram @justin_the_dustbin.
Long Day? Cook This. is his debut cookbook.

ACKNOWLEDGEMENTS

This is something I have been excited to write since the moment this book was given the green light. To give the people their flowers.

Mimi Paul: my wife, partner in crime and biggest critic. You're the main reason I am where I am today. I hope you can forgive me for taking over the kitchen and claiming most of the cupboards (and freezer) as my own. I may or may not have left the kitchen in a state that resembles a natural disaster multiple times, and slacked on the responsibility of house chores (I'm sorry!), but despite all this, I couldn't have done it without you. You were on this journey with me from start to finish – this book is as much yours as it is mine, so thank you for being my biggest supporter and for tolerating all the times I get hangry. You know me better than I do, I love you infinitely and I'm so lucky to have you! P.S. There is such a thing as too much sauce!

To my parents, Annie and Dominic, and little sister, Chloe Tsang, thank you for all the experiences you gave me growing up, and for having such energy and enthusiasm when it comes to cooking and, most importantly, eating! Thank you for keeping me humble and teaching me valuable life lessons and for the love and support you give – all you want for me in life is to be happy. For all the advice you've given me, too – it may not seem as though I listened, but believe me, I did. You taught me to embrace my culture. I love you all so much. I hope I made you proud.

Nancy Paul, my 'I feel sick' sister-in-law, social media adviser and goblin – you pushed me to start this journey, god knows why . . . because you are a kind, loving person? Or maybe because you were hungry? Constant messages telling me to 'start a page' and 'buy a tripod'. Either way, you believed in me, and I wouldn't have done it without you. You now have no excuse to live on a diet of pesto pasta! I hope that one day we will have a conversation that doesn't stray off on a tangent. Thank you for everything! P.S. You will never catch my high five :)

Simon and Louisa Paul, my parents-in-law and my biggest cheerleaders, I feel honoured to be part of your family. You have constantly encouraged me to do things I feel uncomfortable doing, you showed me how to be a good person and how to be on the right side of life, and for that I am grateful. You feed me like a king – I mean, is there any reason to come over other than for food!? Thank you for the belief you've shown in me.

Isabella Bornholt, legendary Arsenal goalkeeper, I was pondering whether to include this as I might never hear the last of it, but here we go. That one little story you posted of me was the catalyst that started everything, leading me to where I am now. I guess everything in life is for a reason! Thank you for your endless support, my day one!

Tessa von Erlach, the NYC queen, I will never forget that cold October night partying in the basement of your Highgate house. That's when you and I were deep in conversation about my newly founded Instagram page, a conversation that I genuinely believe changed the path of my career and opened the door (pun intended) to all this. It might seem small, but you had a vision, which I implemented – all I can say is, it worked! So, thank you from the bottom of my heart.

Sarah Berlingieri, my social media guru and voice note queen, thank you for the never-ending stream of wise and knowledgeable messages! You guided me in a place I was clueless and made me feel confident and comfortable, so thank you!

Ru Merritt: from that random email in February to the phone call giving me the good news, you had the vision from the start – thank you for taking a chance on me. None of this would've been possible without your wisdom and knowledge. You've made my dream come true! P.S. Blue is the new black!

Lucy Kingett, my right hand in all of this, thank you for putting up with my million questions – I seriously couldn't have done it without you. You made sure I met every deadline and had my back throughout! I hope I wasn't too much of a nuisance!

Sam A Harris, what an honour it is to have you as photographer for my book – you are incredibly talented and clearly I made the right choice. Trust me when I say that the images make this book, I couldn't be happier, they are STUNNING!

Sam Dixon, it was a pleasure to have you styling my food. We had many great laughs, even though your chives were rated 6/10 at best (ha ha!). But, if I'm being honest, Big Gus was the real star of the show!

Max Robinson, I couldn't have asked for a better prop stylist. The moment I saw the spread of all things kitchen at the shoot, I knew you nailed it. Everything was me to a tee!

Thank you to Blonder for having the incredible vision for the cover, and to Hannah Naughton for the internal design. The colour palette is perfection and the design is fun, quirky and exactly what I imagined!

Thank you, the entire Ebury team – what an honour it is to be published by you. The amount of work and effort you've put in to create my dream was just incredible. I am so grateful for the passion and excitement you've put into this book.

To all my friends, thank you for being there every step of the way, celebrating and supporting me as this journey unfolded. I could not have done it without you. You bring me so much happiness and joy in life, you are all my favourites (sorry Amelia!). Here's to more pints, hotpots, dances and dinner parties.

Josh Irish, I hope this book will give you some inspiration to cook something other than chicken and rice (and stop you from eating the rice with ketchup – absolutely insane and mildly offensive; Katie, Ruby and Sadie would agree).

Shoutout to Rambo, Luna, Bonnie, Wally and Kitty, our little doubins <3

Ebury Press

UK | USA | Canada | Ireland | Australia
India | New Zealand | South Africa

Ebury Press is part of the Penguin Random House group of companies whose addresses can be found at global.penguinrandomhouse.com

Penguin Random House UK
One Embassy Gardens, 8 Viaduct Gardens, London SW11 7BW

First published by Ebury Press in 2025

3

Copyright © Justin Tsang 2025
Photography © Sam A Harris 2025

The moral right of the author has been asserted.

No part of this book may be used or reproduced in any manner for the purpose of training artificial intelligence technologies or systems. This work is reserved from text and data mining (Article 4(3) Directive (EU) 2019/790).

Editorial Director: Ru Merritt
Project Editor: Lucy Kingett
Production Director: Catherine Ngwong
Cover Designer: Emily Spoors at Blonder Brand
Designer: Hannah Naughton
Photographer: Sam A Harris
Food Stylist: Sam Dixon
Food Stylist Assistants: Lucy Cottle, Allegra D'Agostini, Kristine Jakobsson
Prop Stylist: Max Robinson

Colour origination by Altaimage Ltd
Printed and bound in Germany by Mohn Media Mohndruck GmbH

The authorised representative in the EEA is Penguin Random House Ireland, Morrison Chambers, 32 Nassau Street, Dublin D02 YH68.

A CIP catalogue record for this book is available from the British Library

ISBN 9781529944150

Penguin Random House is committed to a sustainable future for our business, our readers and our planet. This book is made from Forest Stewardship Council® certified paper.

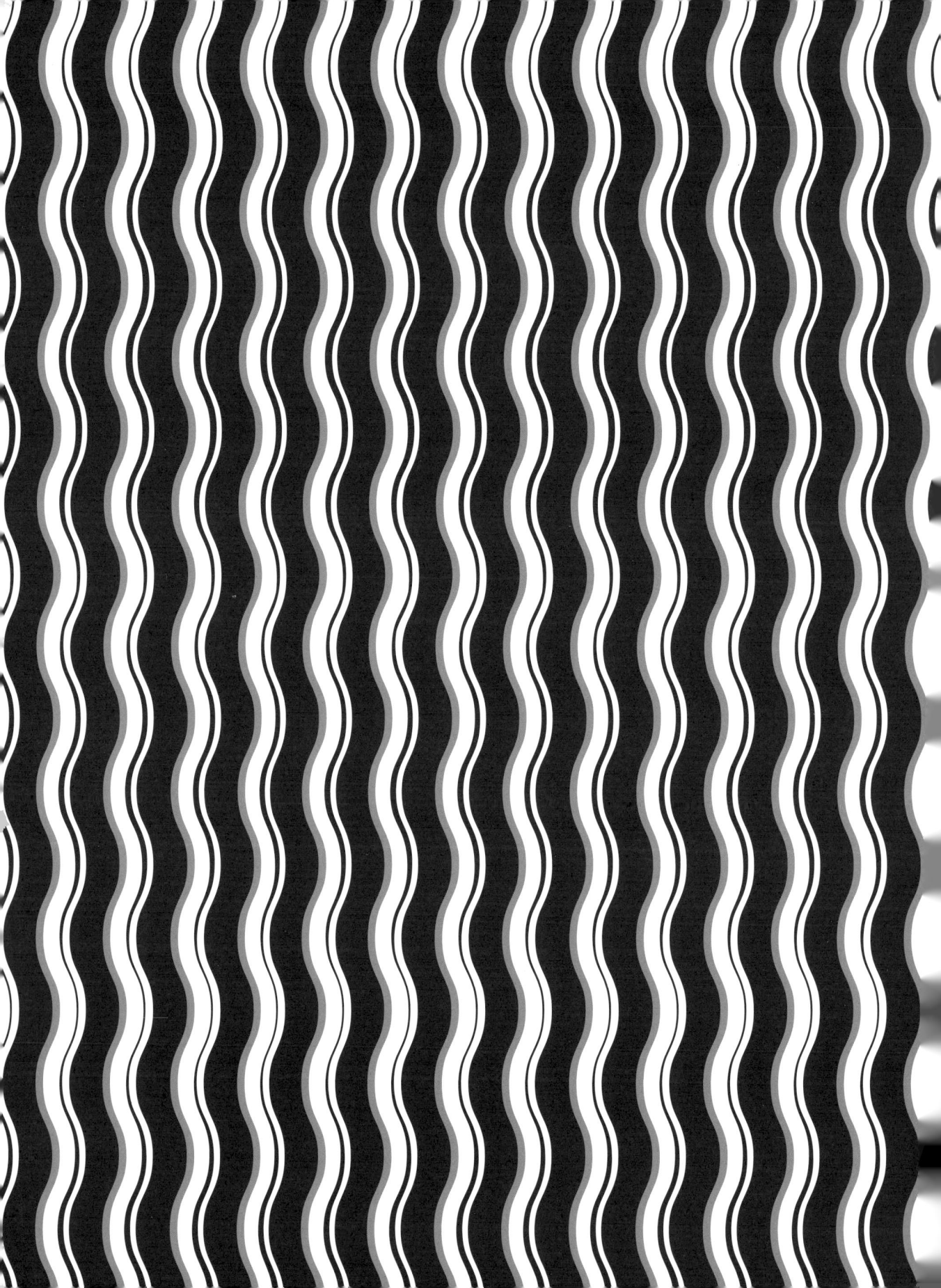